Anti-Semitism

Other Books of Related Interest

Opposing Viewpoints Series

Civil Liberties

Gay Parenting

Racial Profiling

Israel

At Issue Series

Does the World Hate the US?

Should Parents Be Allowed to Choose the Gender
of Their Children?

Should Religious Symbols Be Allowed on Public Land?

Current Controversies Series

Politics and Media

Racism

"Congress shall make no law . . . abridging the freedom of speech, or of the press."

First Amendment to the US Constitution

The basic foundation of our democracy is the First Amendment guarantee of freedom of expression. The Opposing Viewpoints Series is dedicated to the concept of this basic freedom and the idea that it is more important to practice it than to enshrine it.

Anti-Semitism

Noah Berlatsky, Book Editor

GREENHAVEN PRESS
A part of Gale, Cengage Learning

Detroit • New York • San Francisco • New Haven, Conn • Waterville, Maine • London

Elizabeth Des Chenes, *Director, Content Strategy*
Cynthia Sanner, *Publisher*
Douglas Dentino, *Manager, New Product*

For more information, contact:
Greenhaven Press
27500 Drake Rd.
Farmington Hills, MI 48331-3535
Or you can visit our Internet site at gale.cengage.com

Articles in Greenhaven Press anthologies are often edited for length to meet page requirements. In addition, original titles of these works are changed to clearly present the main thesis and to explicitly indicate the author's opinion. Every effort is made to ensure that Greenhaven Press accurately reflects the original intent of the authors. Every effort has been made to trace the owners of copyrighted material.

Cover Image © iStockPhoto.com/YinYang

LIBRARY OF CONGRESS CATALOGING-IN-PUBLICATION DATA

Anti-Semitism / Noah Berlatsky, book editor.
    p. cm. -- (Opposing viewpoints)
    Includes bibliographical references and index.
    ISBN 978-0-7377-6947-0 (hardback) -- ISBN 978-0-7377-6948-7 (paperback)
    1. Antisemitism. I. Berlatsky, Noah.
    DS145.A5995 2014
    305.892'4--dc23
                                        2013037236

Printed in the United States of America
1 2 3 4 5 6 7 18 17 16 15 14

Contents

Chapter 3: Is Opposition to Israeli Policy Linked to Anti-Semitism?

Chapter 4: What Political Groups Are Linked to Anti-Semitism?

Why Consider Opposing Viewpoints?

> *"The only way in which a human being can make some approach to knowing the whole of a subject is by hearing what can be said about it by persons of every variety of opinion and studying all modes in which it can be looked at by every character of mind. No wise man ever acquired his wisdom in any mode but this."*
>
> *John Stuart Mill*

In our media-intensive culture it is not difficult to find differing opinions. Thousands of newspapers and magazines and dozens of radio and television talk shows resound with differing points of view. The difficulty lies in deciding which opinion to agree with and which "experts" seem the most credible. The more inundated we become with differing opinions and claims, the more essential it is to hone critical reading and thinking skills to evaluate these ideas. Opposing Viewpoints books address this problem directly by presenting stimulating debates that can be used to enhance and teach these skills. The varied opinions contained in each book examine many different aspects of a single issue. While examining these conveniently edited opposing views, readers can develop critical thinking skills such as the ability to compare and contrast authors' credibility, facts, argumentation styles, use of persuasive techniques, and other stylistic tools. In short, the Opposing Viewpoints Series is an ideal way to attain the higher-level thinking and reading skills so essential in a culture of diverse and contradictory opinions.

In addition to providing a tool for critical thinking, Opposing Viewpoints books challenge readers to question their own strongly held opinions and assumptions. Most people form their opinions on the basis of upbringing, peer pressure, and personal, cultural, or professional bias. By reading carefully balanced opposing views, readers must directly confront new ideas as well as the opinions of those with whom they disagree. This is not to simplistically argue that everyone who reads opposing views will—or should—change his or her opinion. Instead, the series enhances readers' understanding of their own views by encouraging confrontation with opposing ideas. Careful examination of others' views can lead to the readers' understanding of the logical inconsistencies in their own opinions, perspective on why they hold an opinion, and the consideration of the possibility that their opinion requires further evaluation.

Evaluating Other Opinions

To ensure that this type of examination occurs, Opposing Viewpoints books present all types of opinions. Prominent spokespeople on different sides of each issue as well as well-known professionals from many disciplines challenge the reader. An additional goal of the series is to provide a forum for other, less known, or even unpopular viewpoints. The opinion of an ordinary person who has had to make the decision to cut off life support from a terminally ill relative, for example, may be just as valuable and provide just as much insight as a medical ethicist's professional opinion. The editors have two additional purposes in including these less known views. One, the editors encourage readers to respect others' opinions—even when not enhanced by professional credibility. It is only by reading or listening to and objectively evaluating others' ideas that one can determine whether they are worthy of consideration. Two, the inclusion of such viewpoints encourages the important critical thinking skill of objectively evaluating an author's credentials and bias. This evaluation will illuminate an author's reasons for taking a particular stance on an issue and will aid in readers' evaluation of the author's ideas.

It is our hope that these books will give readers a deeper understanding of the issues debated and an appreciation of the complexity of even seemingly simple issues when good and honest people disagree. This awareness is particularly important in a democratic society such as ours in which people enter into public debate to determine the common good. Those with whom one disagrees should not be regarded as enemies but rather as people whose views deserve careful examination and may shed light on one's own.

Thomas Jefferson once said that "difference of opinion leads to inquiry, and inquiry to truth." Jefferson, a broadly educated man, argued that "if a nation expects to be ignorant and free . . . it expects what never was and never will be." As individuals and as a nation, it is imperative that we consider the opinions of others and examine them with skill and discernment. The Opposing Viewpoints Series is intended to help readers achieve this goal.

David L. Bender and Bruno Leone,
Founders

Introduction

> "It's hard to be a liberal religious Jew
> these days. . . . These days, religion—all
> of it, not just the bomb-wearing, stone-
> throwing kind—has been blamed for ev-
> erything from war to ignorance, racism
> and sexism, even just plain stupidity.
> Oy."
>
> *Jay Michaelson,*
> *"The New Atheism: What's a*
> *Liberal Spiritual Jew to Do?,"*
> Jewish Daily Forward,
> *September 26, 2007*

New atheism is the term for the ideas of a group of modern atheist writers who believe that religion is a singular source of harm to the world and that it should be aggressively refuted. Important new-atheist writers include Richard Dawkins, Sam Harris, and Christopher Hitchens.

New-atheist attacks on religion have led some commentators to accuse the new atheists of bigotry or intolerance. In particular, some new-atheist criticisms of Judaism have led to charges of anti-Semitism. For example, George C. Michalopulos in a February 7, 2011, post at the American Orthodox Institute blog the *Observer* accuses Christopher Hitchens of denying that the Jewish Exodus from Egypt actually historically occurred. Michalopulos says that such "words provide cover to anti-Semites." Michalopulos is also disturbed by Hitchens's defense of the ancient Greek ruler Antiochus, who persecuted the Jews, but who Hitchens sees as simply trying to help the Jews to abandon their "ancient and cruel faith."

Along similar lines, Theodore Sayeed, in a September 4, 2012, post on the website Mondoweiss, charges new-atheist

Sam Harris with blaming the Holocaust on the fact that Jews did not assimilate into German culture. Sayeed points in particular to a statement in Harris's book *The End of Faith* that Jews "brought their troubles upon themselves" through "the content of their own unreasonable, sectarian beliefs."

And finally, new-atheist writer Richard Dawkins was criticized by Lord Sacks, Britain's chief rabbi, for being anti-Semitic. In Dawkins's book *The God Delusion*, he calls the Old Testament God "the most unpleasant character in all fiction." According to John Bingham, writing in a September 14, 2012, article for London's *Daily Telegraph*, Lord Sacks argued that this view of the Old Testament God as immoral was linked to "an anti-Semitic stereotype" long used by Christians and often used to justify violence against Jews.

In response to Lord Sacks's accusation, Dawkins insisted that his views were not anti-Semitic, but "anti-God." Shmarya Rosenberg, in a September 14, 2012, post at the blog *Failed-Messiah.com*, also argues that Dawkins's arguments were not anti-Semitic and says that Lord Sacks had "tarnish[ed] his reputation" by making the accusation.

Other new atheists have also defended Christopher Hitchens from charges of anti-Semitism. Hitchens is actually part Jewish. In a December 21, 2011, article for the *Jewish Daily Forward*, Roane Carey reports that Hitchens discovered his Jewish ancestry only in 1987, when he was thirty-eight years old.

The revelation led him to start meeting regularly with a rabbi, and while he did not renounce his atheism, he did begin to think that, in his words, Judaism "might turn out to be the most ethically sophisticated tributary of humanism." Hitchens is opposed to Zionism (i.e., support of the state of Israel) and Jewish nationalism, but not, Carey says, because he is anti-Semitic but because he believes that Zionism violates the true spirit of Judaism. In fact, Carey says that Hitchens denounced anti-Semitism as "ineradicable and as one element of the toxin with which religion has infected us."

Hitchens's view of anti-Semitism as rooted in religion is shared by other new atheists as well. Sam Harris, for example, has attacked Catholicism for its history of anti-Semitism, including the Inquisition. Harris also frequently condemns what he sees as the anti-Semitism of Islam. In a blog post on March 13, 2012, at his website, for example, Harris argues that Muslim hatred justifies the need for a Jewish state.

> Consider the position of Israel, which is so regularly vilified by the Left. As a secularist and a nonbeliever—and as a Jew—I find the idea of a Jewish state obnoxious. But if ever a state organized around a religion was justified, it is the Jewish state of Israel, given the world's propensity for genocidal anti-Semitism. And if ever criticism of a religious state was unjustified, it is the criticism of Israel that ceaselessly flows from every corner of the Muslim world, given the genocidal aspirations so many Muslims freely confess regarding the Jews. Those who see moral parity between the two sides of Israeli-Palestinian conflict are ignoring rather obvious differences in intent.

The conflicts over new atheism touch on many important themes in the discussion of anti-Semitism. The viewpoints in this book will present other controversies around anti-Semitism in chapters titled *What Social Factors Contribute to Anti-Semitism? What Is the Relationship Among Christianity, Islam, and Anti-Semitism? Is Opposition to Israeli Policy Linked to Anti-Semitism?* and *What Political Groups Are Linked to Anti-Semitism?* In each chapter, different authors will present different viewpoints about whether, and how, anti-Semitism is linked to politics, culture, religion, and society.

OPPOSING
VIEWPOINTS®
SERIES

CHAPTER 1

What Social Factors Contribute to Anti-Semitism?

Chapter Preface

In both Europe and America in recent years, immigration has been a subject of considerable controversy. Commentators have differed sharply in their views of how this concern with immigration has affected anti-Semitism.

On one hand, some writers have argued that opposition to immigration has fed into increased anti-Semitism. In a March 20, 2012, post on his blog *Informed Comment*, Juan Cole, for example, argues that anti-immigrant rhetoric in France uses the same language as anti-Semitism. "French antisemites," Cole writes, "view Jews as foreigners." Thus, when then-president Nicolas Sarkozy declared, "There are too many foreigners in France," he was in part legitimating not only the anti-immigration stance of the far right but its anti-Semitism as well. Along the same lines, in a November 20, 2012, post the Jewish Anti-Defamation League (ADL) noted that the anti-immigrant group Center for Immigration Studies had circulated an e-mail from VDARE, which the ADL called "a racist website . . . known for publishing the work of anti-Semites and white supremacists."

On the other hand, some commentators have argued that it is not anti-immigration, but immigration itself that promotes anti-Semitism. For example, Emerson Vermaat, in a June 6, 2011, article at PipeLineNews.org, argues that increased Muslim immigration to Europe is linked to increased anti-Semitism. Vermaat argues that there have been increases in anti-Semitic incidents in places such as France and Germany because of now larger Muslim populations. He also discusses Sweden, where, he says, the Muslim population has increased from around a thousand in 1970 to four hundred thousand in 2006. Vermaat quotes Swedish historian Mikael Tossavainen:

The largest anti-Semitic incident took place in Stockholm on 18 April 2002, when a rally against anti-Semitism and Islamophobia organized by the Liberal Youth Movement was stormed. Some sixty individuals, mostly of Middle Eastern background, physically attacked participants, destroyed signs and shouted epithets like "Jewish swine!" and "Allahu Akbar! [Great is Allah!]" Many of those in the rally, including some Holocaust survivors, suffered injury and shock before the police intervened after fifteen to twenty minutes. Similar attacks have taken place in Malmö and Göteborg.

Just as people are divided on the relationship between immigration and anti-Semitism, so the links between anti-Semitism and other social factors have also proved controversial. This chapter presents viewpoints examining those links and controversies.

| "Hate ... is part of the culture—the
| way of life—of the society in which it
| exists."

Racism and Anti-Semitism Are Often Culturally Validated

Jack Levin and Jim Nolan

Jack Levin is the Irving and Betty Brudnick Professor of Sociology and Criminology at Northeastern University in Boston; Jim Nolan is an associate professor in the Department of Sociology and Anthropology at West Virginia University. In the following viewpoint, they argue that anti-Semitism, racism, and other forms of prejudice are not the result of aberrant psychology or the demagoguery of charismatic leaders. Rather, they contend that prejudice is often a cultural norm, so that, for example, in Nazi Germany, people who did not support the elimination of the Jews were seen as social rebels and immoral. The authors conclude that cultural norms of prejudice have a major effect on anti-Semitism and racism.

As you read, consider the following questions:

1. According to the authors, why was Hitler able to convince so many Germans to participate in the elimination of Jews?

2. What do Levin and Nolan say is the cultural history of white racism in America?

3. During World War II, why did Jews in Poland and Hungary fare much worse than Jews in Denmark and Belgium, according to the authors?

Given the appropriate conditions, some sympathizers can be moved to dabble in bigotry or even to become hate-mongers. According to [Harvard professor *emeritus* Daniel Jonah] Goldhagen, tens of thousands of German citizens during the Nazi era of the 1930s, reacting to Hitler's interpretation of a terrible economic situation, translated their sympathy for anti-Semitism into mass murder.

At the Nuremberg War Crimes Trials, defendants sought unsucessfully to elude responsibility for their participation in the Nazi slaughter by arguing they had been mesmerized into obeying the orders of a charismatic Adolph Hitler. Rather than admit that they approved of what he represented, they spoke instead of Hitler's domineering presence, his irresistible magnetism, his ability to cast a hypnotic spell. Their defense was meant to let them off the hook: "No Hitler, no Holocaust."

According to [history professor John] Weiss, even the most powerful orators cannot possibly convert those who have not already bought into their ideas. Radical demagogues have the capacity to confirm but not to convince. It was not Hitler's style so much as the substance of his rhetoric that persuaded hundreds of thousands of German citizens to participate in, or at the very least not to oppose, the massacre of Jews.

Of course, there may be some limited circumstances, for example, among prisoners of war, where the control over an individual is absolute or complete. Under such conditions, it may actually be appropriate to speak in terms of "brainwashing," "mind control," or "thought reform." But in most of the circumstances of everyday life, individuals possess an element of free will that can only be manipulated so much. The most authoritarian and charismatic leader cannot completely undermine individual autonomy and voluntarism. In fact, it is pure myth to suggest that the members of a society collectively lack any power to resist while under the spell of a madman. Even extremely vulnerable individuals possess an "active self" that severely limits the power of the most persuasive leader to mold or shape the behavior and beliefs of his followers.

Cultural Hate

It would be comforting if we were able to characterize hate and prejudice as deviant, irrational, and pathological behavior—as an aspect of the domain of a few "crazies" on the fringe of society whose psychosis is in urgent need of treatment by psychotherapy, psychotropic medications, or both. Unfortunately, hate hardly depends for its existence on individual pathology or abnormal psychology. Nor is it a form of deviance from the point of view of mainstream society. Even if the admission of being prejudiced is unacceptable, hate itself is instead normal, rational, and conventional. It is part of the culture—the way of life—of the society in which it exists, appealing typically to the most conventional and traditional of its members.

Even in such an extreme set of circumstances as the atrocities committed under Nazism, genocide was carried out and encouraged not by ideological fanatics and schizophrenics but by ordinary citizens. Even the perpetrators were normal by conventional mental health standards. The power of Nazism was indeed strong, but it hardly prevented most ordinary citizens from making ethical decisions and functioning in a normal way. For example, Polish authorities suggested for decades that the Nazis had been responsible for a 1941 massacre of the Jewish residents of the town of Jedwabne. New evidence ar-

Estimated Number of Jews Murdered During World War II

Country	Pre-War Jewish Population	Estimated Murdered
Austria	185,000	50,000
Belgium	66,000	25,000
Bohemia/Moravia	118,000	78,000
Bulgaria	50,000	0
Denmark	8,000	60
Estonia	4,500	2,000
Finland	2,000	7
France	350,000	77,000
Germany	565,000	142,000
Greece	75,000	65,000
Hungary	825,000	550,000
Italy	44,500	7,500
Latvia	91,500	70,000
Lithuania	168,000	140,000
Luxembourg	3,500	1,000
Netherlands	140,000	100,000
Norway	1,700	762
Poland	3,300,000	3,000,000
Romania	609,000	270,000
Slovakia	89,000	71,000
Soviet Union	3,020,000	1,000,000
Yugoslavia	78,000	60,000
Total	9,793,700	5,709,329

TAKEN FROM: Jennifer Rosenberg, "How Many Jews Were Murdered?," *About.com*. http://history1900s.about.com.

gued that it was not Nazi soldiers but ordinary Polish farmers who herded 1,600 of their Jewish neighbors into a barn and set it on fire.

The Normality of Hate

Where it is cultural, sympathy for a particular hatred may become a widely shared and enduring element in the normal state of affairs of a group of people. Even more important, the prejudice may become systematically organized to reward individuals who are bigoted and cruel and to punish those individuals who are caring and respectful of differences. In such circumstances, tolerance for group differences may actually be regarded as rebellious behavior and those who openly express tolerance may be viewed as rebels.

Sympathizers draw their hate from the culture, developing it from an early age. As a cultural phenomenon, racism is as American as apple pie. It has been around for centuries and is learned by every generation in the same way that our most cherished cultural values have been acquired: around the dinner table; through books and television programs; from teachers, friends, and relatives.

In the American experience, White racism has a long and deep cultural history, being traceable back centuries to the impetus in the New World for enslaving large numbers of Africans rather than White Europeans. Racism can therefore be seen not as a conscious conspiracy of powerful people or the delusional thinking of a few radical bigots. Rather, it is an important, if largely unconscious, aspect of America's historical experience and of our shared cultural order, arising from the taken-for-granted assumptions that Americans learn to make about themselves and others.

Stereotyping also seems to have a cultural basis that is dependent on the cognitive development of an individual. As a result, the particular cultural images of a group of people may not be accepted, or even understood, by a child until long after she has already developed an intense hatred toward its members.

Later on, education seems to be effective in reducing stereotyped thinking. In addition, legislation can, within limits, reduce discriminatory behavior. Yet, the emotional component of hate may persevere over the course of a lifetime, regardless of attempts to modify it. Beginning so early in life, hate may become a passion for the individual who acquires it, being much harder to modify than stereotypes or the tendency to discriminate.

The Cultural Breadth of Hate

The cultural element of hate can be seen in its amazing ability to sweep across broad areas of a nation. Individuals separated by region, age, social class, and ethnic background all tend to share roughly the same stereotyped images of various groups. In the United States, for example, some degree of anti-Black, anti-Asian, and anti-Latino racism can be found among substantial segments of Americans—males and females, young and old, rich and poor—from New York to California, from North Dakota to Texas.

Similarly, in Nazi Germany, Hitler's condemnation of the Jews reflected not only his personal opinion, but also the beliefs of hundreds of thousands of German and Austrian citizens. While the police looked on approvingly, university students joined together to beat and batter their Jewish classmates. Faculty members and students voiced demands to rid the universities of Jews and cosponsored lectures on "the Jewish problem." Because of their genuine conviction, thousands of German soldiers and police helped to murder Jews. Civil service bureaucrats aided in doing the paperwork to expedite carrying out Hitler's extermination program. Many important business, banking, and industrial firms cooperated in the task of enslaving and murdering Jewish citizens. Thousands of German physicians cooperated in sterilizing or eliminating the "undesirables." Finally, whereas the church in other European countries denounced racist anti-Semitism, Germany's religious leaders (both Catholic and Protestant) failed to protest the final solution [i.e., exterminating the Jews].

At the cultural level, the emotional character of racial or religious hatred is reflected collectively in laws and norms that prohibit intimate contact between different groups of people. In the Deep South, Jim Crow laws created separate public facilities: "colored" and "White" restrooms, waiting rooms, water fountains, and sections on public buses. In the South African version of apartheid [racial segregation], Blacks were similarly restricted to living in segregated communities and could work among Whites only under the strictest supervision.

In Nazi Germany, the same sort of enduring sympathy for hate might be found among citizens concerning anti-Semitism. In explaining the particular stronghold of Hitler's "final solution," Goldhagen has argued that an "eliminationist anti-Semitism" was a long-standing feature of German culture that dated back centuries. The majority of ordinary German citizens believed that the Jews, ostensibly being responsible for all of their country's economic woes, had to be eliminated at any cost. Thus, rather than some dark and repulsive secret, gruesome stories about the Nazi's brutal anti-Jewish policies—the death camps, gas chambers, hideous experiments, and mass murders—were told and retold proudly across the land to ordinary German citizens who were eager to hear them.

Nazi anti-Semitism was located at the end of a continuum of cultural bigotry that seems to have helped determine the fate of Jews not only in Germany but in other European countries as well. Nations such as Poland and Hungary, which had a long-standing tradition of anti-Semitic attitudes and behavior, were also nations in which a large proportion of Jews were murdered; countries such as Denmark, Belgium, and

Bulgaria where a tradition of tolerance and respect for religious diversity was strong were also countries where a relatively sizable proportion of Jews survived.

"Worldwide, the rhetoric of homophobia recapitulates the tropes of classical Jew hatred."

Is Homophobia the New Anti-Semitism?

Michelle Goldberg

Michelle Goldberg is a senior correspondent at the American Prospect. *In the following viewpoint, she argues that an anti-gay movement is becoming an international system of hatred similar to anti-Semitism. She points out that Jews and gays are both often associated with modernity, and such stereotypes are used as an excuse for hatred by national, Christian, and Islamic religious traditionalists. She says that international homophobia must be met with international action and activism by supporters of gay rights.*

As you read, consider the following questions:

1. According to Goldberg's summation of news reports, how was the May 2009 gay-rights protest in Moscow quashed before it could begin?

2. What does Hossein Alizadeh, as cited by the author, identify as the two major sources of homophobic thought globally?

3. Who is Scott Lively, and how is he important to the global anti-gay movement, according to Goldberg?

On May 17, 1990, the World Health Organization removed homosexuality from its list of mental disorders. That's why gay-rights activists chose May 17 for the International Day Against Homophobia, a worldwide series of events, now in its fourth year, designed to spotlight the terrible abuses gay and lesbian people face in much of the world. In what might be seen as a prescient tribute to Larry Craig, it goes by the acronym IDAHO. Even before this year's IDAHO began on Sunday, events in Moscow offered a lurid demonstration of why global homophobia needs our attention.

Moscow gay-rights activists had planned a march to coincide with the finale of the ultra-campy Eurovision Song Contest on Saturday. It was a brave and risky undertaking—in the past, gay-rights demonstrators in Russia have been met with violence from both police and right-wing thugs. Moscow's mayor has called gay-rights marches "satanic," and his spokesperson told journalists that the activists threatened "not only to destroy the moral pillars of our society but also to deliberately provoke disorder, which would threaten the lives and security of Muscovites and guests of the city." *The Independent* [London] reported that organizers hid out in a country house to avoid arrest in the days leading up to the march, then dodged police roadblocks to make it into the city.

In the end, the protest was quashed before it could begin. "The demonstration lasted for about a minute before the police set upon them from all sides, clambering through the shrubs and knocking news cameramen out of the way to seize the demonstrators, pin their arms behind their backs and drag them off into waiting buses and patrol wagons," reported the

Los Angeles Times. Added *The Telegraph* [London], "Some activists were detained for doing little more than talking to reporters, including a female campaigner who had her glasses and shoes torn off and her dress pulled up above her waist as she was carried screaming into a bus." Far-right anti-gay demonstrators were allowed to have their own event elsewhere in the city.

As the organizers of IDAHO know, this kind of official repression is all too common. Opposition to homosexuality in conservative countries is, of course, nothing new. But right now, partly in response to the increasing visibility of gay rights in the West, we're seeing a ratcheting up of anti-gay demagoguery and persecution throughout the world.

The hatred comes in many guises and from many different directions. But there are some underlying themes, enough so that it's possible to talk about global homophobia as a single concept, akin to anti-Semitism. Indeed, worldwide, the rhetoric of homophobia recapitulates the tropes of classical Jew hatred. Gay people are seen as a subversive internal enemy with dangerous international connections. Even in places where they've been cowed into near invisibility, they're viewed as having an almost occult power. They represent modernism and cosmopolitanism, the bete noirs [French for "black beasts," in English it connotes a hated object] of every type of fundamentalism.

In part, global homophobia is a reaction to the great strides the gay-rights movement has made internationally. Almost every developed nation—including, once Obama took office, the United States—signed onto a recent United Nations declaration calling for the decrimalization of homosexuality worldwide. The European Union's Charter of Fundamental Rights recognizes gay rights. In 2006, at a conference that led to the creation of the International Day Against Homophobia, Louise Arbour, then the U.N.'s high commissioner for human rights, denounced anti-gay legislation in forceful terms and dismissed the kind of cultural relativist arguments often used to justify repressive laws.

"In my view," she said, "respect for cultural diversity is insufficient to justify the existence of laws that violate the fundamental right to life, security, and privacy by criminalizing harmless private relations between consenting adults. Even when such laws are not actively enforced, or worse when they are arbitrarily enforced, their mere existence fosters an atmosphere of fear, silence, and denial of identity in which LGBT persons are confined."

Meanwhile, just as the gay-rights movement has been globalized, so has the religious opposition. "There are currently two major sources of homophobic thought globally," says Hossein Alizadeh, the Iranian-born communications coordinator of the International Gay and Lesbian Human Rights Commission. "One is primarily Christian conservative movements that are mainly based in the United States. We see a lot of that fitting into the hatred and violence in Africa, the missionaries that go into different African countries and bring with them the message of hate. The second is Islamic fundamentalism."

In many Muslim countries, homosexuality is denounced as a decadent and imperialistic imposition. "Almost on a weekly basis you see there's some sort of article published in the Muslim world blaming the United Nations for promoting homosexuality and basically destroying the fabric of the society," Alizadeh says. Indeed, such rhetoric sometimes comes from the anti-colonialist left as well as the religious right. In a 2002 article on what he called the "Gay International," Columbia University professor Joseph Massad presented the global gay-rights movement as an instrument of Western hegemony. "Following in the footsteps of the white Western women's movement, which had sought to universalize its issues through imposing its own colonial feminism on the women's move-

The Nazi Attack on Homosexuals

Homosexuality, the Nazis charged, weakened Germany in several ways. It was accused of being a factor in the declining birthrate that threatened to leave the nation unable to sustain itself. It was also feared as an "infection" that could become an "epidemic," particularly among the nation's vulnerable youth. It was thought that it could give rise to a dangerous state-within-the-state since homosexuals were believed to form self-serving groups. It endangered public morality and contributed to the decline of the community. For the good of the state, the Nazis asserted, homosexuality had to be eradicated.

United States Holocaust Memorial Museum,
"Nazi Persecution of Homosexuals, 1933–1945."
www.ushmm.org.

ments in the non-Western world . . . the gay movement has adopted a similar missionary role," he wrote.

In Iraq, the scapegoating of gays and lesbians as agents of the West has been particularly deadly. "The country was invaded back in 2003, and ever since then things have been going south rather than getting better," Alizadeh says. "People have to blame somebody, and gays seem to be the easiest target. There are lots of comments about how homosexuality did not exist in Iraq before the U.S. invasion. People think the least they can do in order to protect their culture is just to go after gay people and kill them."

Terrible abuses of gays and lesbians are certainly not limited to the Muslim world. In Africa, despite the near-invisibility of gay people on much of the continent, there's a full-blown gay panic underway, much of it stoked by evangelicals with ties to the American right. Last month [April 2009],

Burundi passed draconian anti-gay legislation, making gay sex punishable by up to two years in prison. Nigeria is currently considering a bill that would criminalize the "coming together of persons of the same sex with the purpose of leaving [sic] together as husband and wife or for other purposes of same sexual relationship." In Uganda, where same-sex relations are already punishable by life in prison, Christian-right organizations have been accusing homosexuals of "recruitment," leading to calls for even more punitive anti-gay legislation.

Scott Lively, a key figure in the global anti-gay movement, spoke in Uganda in March. Indeed, wherever one sees really furious Christian anti-gay activism, one often sees his name. Lively is the co-author of a book called *The Pink Swastika*, which posits that Nazism was a homosexual movement and that the modern gay-rights movement is its direct descendent. He's also written a book called *The Poisoned Stream*, a kind of anti-gay *Protocols of the Elders of Zion*, which traces the machinations of "a dark and powerful homosexual presence" through "the Spanish Inquisition, the French 'Reign of Terror,' the era of South African apartheid, and the two centuries of American Slavery."

Lively has been particularly influential in the former Soviet Union. "*The Pink Swastika* has become Lively's passport to fame among anti-gay church leaders and their followers in Eastern Europe, as well as Russian-speaking anti-gay activists in America," reported the Southern Poverty Law Center in 2007. "Lively frequently speaks about the book and his broader anti-gay agenda in churches, police academies, and television news studios throughout the former Soviet Union."

Lively is close to Pastor Alexey Ledyaev, whose New Generation Church, an influential megachurch based in Riga, Latvia, has satellites all over the region. As the SPLC reported, he's known for staging large-scale Christian rock operas "replete with lasers, smoke machines, and spandex-clad actors in ghoulish makeup. One of the rock operas, which young

Russian-speaking anti-gay activists promote on video-sharing web sites, features a hero character wearing a tuxedo battling men in black tights armed with tiki torches. Over heavy-metal guitar riffs, a military-like chorus sings of 'victory over the gays.'"

This aggressive, even obsessive homophobia, more than simple religious traditionalism, is the context for the violence in Moscow on Saturday [at the quashed pride rally]. Anti-gay bigotry, like anti-Semitism, has its local particularities everywhere it surfaces, but it's also increasingly part of a bigger phenomenon, one knit together by overarching conspiracy theories. The activists behind IDAHO have made an important start in publicizing the international character of the problem. Worldwide, those most fervently opposed to gay rights are organizing across borders. The people standing up to them need to do so as well.

> *"It is an iron-clad rule in the history of group relations: the majority's toleration of every minority lessens with the worsening of the majority's condition."*

Anti-Semitism Is Worse During an Economic Crisis

Ira Stoll

Ira Stoll is the editor of FutureofCapitalism.com and the author of Samuel Adams: A Life. *In the following viewpoint, he argues that Jews have frequently faced increased anti-Semitism and persecution during times of economic hardship. This has occurred even when Jews have been assimilated and have held important political and professional positions, as they did in Germany prior to the Nazi takeover. Stoll adds that Jews are often stereotypically associated with capitalism and so may be singled out for blame during downturns. He concludes that American Jews are not immune from anti-Semitism and that threats and signs of persecution should be taken seriously.*

As you read, consider the following questions:

1. What does Stoll say may have been the causes of the First Crusade?

2. What does the author quote Friedrich Hayek as saying that National Socialism was an attack on?

3. Who is Hassan Nasrallah, as described by Stoll, and why does Stoll say his comments on the Jews are especially chilling?

Walking down the street in my solidly upper-middle-class New York City neighborhood the other day was a neatly dressed man angrily cursing into his cell phone about "Jew Wall Street bankers."

I was headed in the opposite direction and didn't stop to interview him about his particular grievances, but the brief encounter crystallized for me a foreboding that the financial crisis [that began in 2008] may trigger a new outbreak of anti-Semitism.

It is a fear that is being articulated ever more widely. President Bill Clinton's secretary of labor, Robert Reich, frets on his blog, "History shows how effective demagogic ravings can be when a public is stressed economically." He warns that Jews, along with gays and blacks, could become victims of populist rage.

In the New York *Jewish Week* newspaper, a column by Rabbi Ronald Price of the Union for Traditional Judaism begins, "In the 1930s, as Germany's economy collapsed, the finger was pointed at the Jews and the Nazis ascended to power. The famous Dreyfus Affair [at the turn of the twentieth century], in which a Jew was falsely accused of treason in France, followed on the heels of economic turmoil."

At this juncture, the trepidation may yet seem like paranoia, or special pleading akin to the old joke about the newspaper headline, "World Ends in Nuclear Attack: Poor, Minorities Hardest Hit." Everyone is feeling the brunt of the recession; why worry about the Jews in particular? After all, Jews today have two refuges: Israel and America, a land where Jews have attained remarkable power and prosperity and have a constitutionally protected right to exercise their religion freely. In that case, why worry about potential danger to the Jews at all?

One answer is that the historical precedents are exceedingly grim. The causes of the First Crusade, in which thousands of Jews were murdered, are still being debated, but some historians link it to famine and a poor harvest in 1095. As for the expulsion of the Jews from Spain in 1492, the foremost historian of its causes, Benzion Netanyahu (the father of Israel's new prime minister), writes of the desire of the persecutors "to get rid of their debts by getting rid of their creditors." More generally, he writes, "it is an iron-clad rule in the history of group relations: the majority's toleration of every minority lessens with the worsening of the majority's condition."

Jews Are at Risk

Lest this seem overly crude economic determinism, consider that the Jews have been victims not only of unrest prompted by economic distress but of attempts to remedy such economic distress with socialism. Take it from Friedrich Hayek, the late Nobel Prize winning Austrian economist. In *The Road to Serfdom*, Hayek wrote, "In Germany and Austria the Jew had come to be regarded as the representative of Capitalism." Thus, the response in those countries, National Socialism, was an attack on both capitalism and the Jews.

There are ample indicators of current anti-Semitic attitudes. A poll conducted recently in Europe by the Anti-Defamation League found 74% of Spaniards believe Jews "have too much power in international financial markets," while 67% of Hungarians believe Jews "have too much power in the business world." Here in America, the Web site of *National Journal* is hosting an "expert blog" by former CIA official Michael Scheuer, now a professor at Georgetown, complaining of a "fifth column of pro-Israel U.S. citizens" who are "unquestionably enemies of America's republican experiment."

Jews and Economic Success

For Jews, Jewish economic success has long been a source of both pride and embarrassment. For centuries, Jewish economic success led anti-Semites to condemn capitalism as a form of Jewish domination and exploitation, or to attribute Jewish success to unsavory qualities of the Jews themselves. The anti-Semitic context of such discussions led Jews to downplay the reality of their economic achievement—except in internal conversations. Moreover, for most people, the workings of advanced capitalist economies are opaque and difficult to comprehend. When economic times are bad and people are hurting, some inevitably search for a more easily grasped, concrete target on which to pin their ill fortunes. That target has often been the Jews. Even today, some Jews regard the public discussion of Jews and capitalism as intrinsically impolitic, as if conspiratorial fantasies about Jews and money can be eliminated by prudent silence.

Jerry Z. Muller,
Capitalism and the Jews, 2010.

And over at *Yahoo! Finance,* the message board discussing [the failed brokerage firm] Goldman Sachs is rife with comments about "Jew pigs" and the "Zionist Federal Reserve."

So will the Jews come under attack? The existence of the Jewish state guarantees refuge for Jews around the world, but it carries with it its own risks. Hezbollah's [an Islamic militant group in Lebanon] leader, Hassan Nasrallah, has said that if the Jews "all gather in Israel, it will save us the trouble of going after them world-wide." It's a comment all the more chilling as Nasrallah's Iranian sponsors are on the brink of making a nuclear bomb.

As for the idea that Jewish professional, political, and economic success in America is a guarantee of security, that, too, has its risks. As Yuri Sleskine recounted in his book *The Jewish Century*, in 1900 Vienna more than half of the lawyers, doctors and professional journalists were Jewish, as were 70% of the members of the stock exchange. In Germany, after World War I but before the Nazis came to power, Jews served as finance minister and as foreign minister. Such achievements have a way of being fleeting.

It may yet be that the Jews escape the current economic crisis having only lost fortunes. But if not, there will have been no lack of warning about the threat. When Jews gather Wednesday [April 2009] night for the Passover Seder, we will recite the words from the Hagadah, the book that relays the Israelite exodus from slavery in Egypt: "In every generation they rise up against us to destroy us." This year, they will resonate all the more ominously.

> *"Blood-curdling anti-Semitism is less likely to come from blacks than, as it always has—if at all—from. . .white right-wing populism."*

Anti-Semitism Among African Americans Was Based on Cultural Factors That Have Now Changed

Jim Sleeper

Jim Sleeper is a lecturer in politicial science at Yale University and the author of Liberal Racism. *In the following viewpoint, he argues that expressions of anti-Semitism by some black leaders in the 1990s were both aberrant and rooted in inner-city experiences in which Jewish merchants and social service providers were the most visible whites in black areas. Sleeper argues that those experiences have faded as more blacks have moved into the middle class and generally have become more integrated into mainstream America. He concludes that black anti-Semitism is not a real threat to Jews.*

As you read, consider the following questions:

1. According to Sleeper, why did blacks sometimes target Jews, if not because of Jews' vulnerability?

2. How has the election of Barack Obama changed the relationship between blacks and Jews, in the author's opinion?

3. How has 9/11 changed the position of blacks in American society, according to Sleeper?

Early in the 1990s—so many years ago that it's nowhere to be found online—I was on a panel about black anti-Semitism at New York's 92nd Street Y, where the historian of slavery Eugene Genovese observed that if a black demagogue called Italian Americans "racists," they'd come after him with baseball bats, but if he called Jews "racists," they'd hold a few conferences at the 92nd Street Y.

Genovese was hinting that while the bat wielders weren't right, neither were liberal Jews, who compulsively professed sympathy for blacks gripped by politics of racial paroxysm. A lot was wrong with liberal professions of "understanding" of the rhetoric of City College of New York Afrocentrist Leonard Jeffries or Nation of Islam leader Louis Farrakhan, to say nothing of the anti-white rhetoric surrounding the hate crime at Howard Beach, [and of] the trials of Tawana Brawley and O.J. Simpson,[1] and other cases of the time.

But something was wrong, too, with the compulsive alarm about black anti-Semitism that consumed some Jews, and when it came my turn to speak, I explained, as I would later in writing, why black demagogues in New York couldn't be compared to Berlin ranters in the late 1920s. For some blacks,

1. Three black men were assaulted by a group of whites in Howard Beach, New York, in 1986; Tawana Brawley is an African American woman who falsely accused six white men of raping her in 1987; O.J. Simpson is an African American football star acquitted in 1995 of murdering his white wife and her friend.

Jews were just "white folks whose skin they could get under," not because Jews were so vulnerable, but because they were more likely to react as humanely as Genovese suggested.

At the panel, I told of how, amid a long, ugly black boycott of some Korean stores in Brooklyn at the time, I'd asked an ageing Jewish community-relations man for his assessment.

"Oh, s'wonderful, s'wonderful," he'd said.

"Huh?" I'd responded. "What's s'wonderful?"

"Well, the merchants aren't Jewish, so the protesters aren't taking potshots at us there. And the mayor's not Jewish, like Ed Koch. We can be like the Quakers now; we can mediate!" he said, opening his palms with a hamish peacemaking gesture.

[Author] Saul Bellow, sitting there in the audience at the Y, threw back his head and laughed silently, appreciatively. [Author] Cynthia Ozick looked less amused at my suggestion that Jews weren't on a slippery slope to Auschwitz just because Jeffries and Farrakhan, whom most whites despise, broke a taboo against anti-Semitic rhetoric.

It's clearer now that blood-curdling anti-Semitism is less likely to come from blacks than, as it always has—if at all—from the white right-wing populism, with which some neoconservative Jews allied themselves until recently. Blacks aren't the problem, for several reasons.

Blacks Are Not the Problem

First, blacks' own orientations within American society have changed since the 1990s.

Although racism and poverty are still powerful, so is the maturation and—dare one say—the integration of a black middle class that while imperiled now (as are many whites) by economic crisis, has few memories of conflicts with those Jewish merchants, landlords, caseworkers and teachers who once dominated black neighborhoods. Jeffries and Farrakhan took their listeners back into a psychic landscape flickering with old, familiar Jewish demons. It's fading now, as my Jewish community-relations man and Bellow understood.

Second, for all the bigotry against President [Barack] Obama, his election [in 2008], with more white votes than black ones, has reoriented many blacks' feelings of American belonging. His Jewish support, the highest of any white group, makes Jews something more than just "white folks whose skin you can get under."

Third, immigrants to the United States from majority-black societies abroad are less—or some of them very differently—obsessed with the psychic as well as physical cruelties of slavery and segregation. That Obama himself is not a descendant of American slaves reinforces this shift in blacks' own understandings of their blackness.

Fourth, Jewish orientations have changed, too. The 9/11 [2001] attacks shifted many whites' (and Jews') fears away from black dysfunction and toward Muslim subversion. You needn't share the anti-Muslim sentiment—I consider most of it folly—to be glad that blacks are more accepted by whites, as allies against domestic and foreign terrorism.

Finally, the neoconservatives, who led the Jewish obsession with black anti-Semitism after the late 1960s and then the shift to obsessing about Muslim anti-Semitism after 9/11, have been significantly discredited for overplaying both hands—in a war-mongering foreign policy, as in inflating the implications of black anger.

For example, Yale University, where I teach, recently and quite rightly disbanded its neocon-heavy Institute for the Interdisciplinary Study of Antisemitism, which more accurately could have been called the "Institute for Jewish Nationalism and War With Iran."

Demagoguery is never justifiable. In the 1990s I was a leader in chronicling and condemning much of what passed for black "civil rights" activism as destructive of public trust. But as early as that conference at the 92nd Street Y, I understood that Jews, too, can get carried away by fears that have deep historical resonance but are all-too-easily misdirected.

Periodical and Internet Sources Bibliography

The following articles have been selected to supplement the diverse views presented in this chapter.

Daniel Finkelstein	"Cultural Roots of Antisemitism," *Jewish Chronicle Online*, June 10, 2011. www.thejc.com/comment-and-debate/columnists/50034/cultural-roots-antisemitism.
Daniel Greenfield	"Anti-Semitism Is Racism," *Frontpage*, May 9, 2012. http://frontpagemag.com/2012/dgreenfield/anti-semitism-is-racism.
Christopher Hitchens	"Chosen," *Atlantic Monthly*, September 2010.
Public Broadcasting System	"From Swastika to Jim Crow: Black-Jewish Relations," n.d. www.pbs.org/itvs/fromswastikatojimcrow/relations_2.html.
Hannah Rosenthal	"Remarks on Anti-Semitism and Human Rights for LGBT People for the Cream City Foundation," US State Department, May 30, 2012. www.state.gov/j/drl/rls/rm/2012/191574.htm.
Christopher Shea	"Anti-Semitism and the Financial Crisis," *Boston Globe*, May 13, 2009. www.boston.com/bostonglobe/ideas/brainiac/2009/05/antisemitism_an.html.
Utne Reader	"Anti-Semitism in the Economic Crisis," September–October 2009. www.utne.com/Politics/Anti-Semitism-Economic-Crisis-Recession.aspx.
Danielle Wiener-Bronner	"'Why Do People Hate Jews?' Is Not the Right Question," *Huffington Post Blog*, May 30, 2012. www.huffingtonpost.com/danielle-wienerbronner/why-do-people-hate-jews-blodget_b_1554745.html.

CHAPTER 2

What Is the Relationship Among Christianity, Islam, and Anti-Semitism?

Chapter Preface

The evangelical Christian community has had a particularly intense and in some cases controversial relationship with Jews. Early-twentieth-century fundamentalist churches were sometimes associated with anti-Semitism, and even as recently as 1976, renowned University of Chicago historian of religions Martin E. Marty noted that evangelical fundamentalist churches were more likely to be anti-Semitic than were liberal Protestant churches.

However, in more recent years many evangelicals have become intensely pro-Jewish and even—or, perhaps, especially—pro-Israel. In part, this support is rooted in the Old Testament description of the Jews as God's chosen people, or as a 2006 *Washington Post* article quotes conservative Christian pastor Lamarr Mooneyham as putting it: "This term that keeps coming up in the Old Book—the Chosen, the Chosen. . . . I'm a pardoned gentile, but I'm not one of the Chosen People. They're the apple of [God's] eye."

But such evangelical support for Jews, however, is rooted in more complicated theological reasoning. Evangelical Christian theology embraces what is known as dispensationalism, which holds that the "end times" of the world, when Jesus is expected to return, will see a worldwide conversion to Christianity and will occur only when the Jews have returned to Israel. Some evangelical support for Israel, then, is an effort to bring about the promised end of the world—and the promised conversion of the Jews to Christianity.

Jews have thus been divided about how to respond to evangelical enthusiasm for the state of Israel. Julie Galambush, a former American Baptist who converted to Judaism, was also quoted in the above-mentioned *Post* article. According to Galambush, evangelicals' desire to help Jews is sincere yet at the same time, "believing that someday Jews will stop being

Jews and become Christians is still a form of hoping that someday there will be no more Jews"—which could be considered a form of anti-Semitism.

Some Jews, however, have enthusiastically embraced evangelical support for Israel. Abraham Foxman, national director of the Anti-Defamation League, has stated that Israel is in an embattled position and needs US help to survive and that therefore, "these realities should make American Jews highly appreciative of the incredible support that the State of Israel gets from a significant group of Americans—the Evangelical Christian Right." Similarly, Keith Pavlischek, in a 2008 article in the religious journal *First Things*, encourages Jews and evangelicals to work together against the anti-Semitic and anti-Zionist ideologies of Islam. Jews, Pavlischek suggests, should "accept the friendship of Christians who share their perspective on a dearly held foreign policy issue."

Evangelicals are of course not the only religious group with a controversial relationship with anti-Semitism. The rest of this chapter presents conflicting viewpoints on the relationships among Christianity, Islam, and attitudes toward Jews.

> "Over the centuries many discrimina-
> tory measures have been taken in
> Christian environments against Jews.
> The infrastructure for this was laid in
> the early history of Christianity."

Anti-Semitism Has Christian Roots

Pieter van der Horst, as told to Manfred Gerstenfeld

Pieter van der Horst is professor emeritus *of Jewish studies at Utrecht University.* Manfred Gerstenfeld *is the author of numerous books, including* Judging the Netherlands: The Renewed Holocaust Restitution Process. *In the following viewpoint by Gerstenfeld, he quotes heavily from an interview with van der Horst, who argues that Jesus saw himself as Jewish and, as cited by three of the four New Testament Gospels, made few if any anti-Semitic statements. Christian writings of a later date, however, do contain anti-Semitic references to Jews as the children of devils or as the killers of Christ, and these references have been used as a basis for persecution of Jews. Van der Horst concludes that anti-Semitic persecution has its roots in early Christian tradition.*

As you read, consider the following questions:

1. According to van der Horst, why did the Jews see it as terrible that Christians were equating Jesus with God?

2. What political reasons does van der Horst say that the evangelist Matthew probably had for absolving Pilate of guilt in the death of Christ?

3. What are church father John Chrysostom's most notorious writings, according to van der Horst?

"Christian anti-Semitism began much later than Jesus' life. In the Gospels of Matthew, Mark, and Luke, which are the historically more reliable ones, Jesus views himself as a messenger of God to the Jews and as a member of the Jewish people. He wanted to prepare them for what he saw as the approaching end of time and God's imminent kingdom. Jesus was not planning to initiate a new religion. The writer of a later book, the Gospel of John, has Jesus make anti-Semitic remarks. That book, however, is much less historical."

Prof. Pieter van der Horst studied classical philology and literature. In 1978, he received his PhD in theology from Utrecht University. After his studies, he taught the literature and history of early Christianity and Judaism. Prof. van der Horst is a member of the Royal Netherlands Academy of Arts and Sciences.

He remarks: "In the three more historically based earlier Gospels, one sees Jesus in fierce dispute with leaders of the various Jewish groups, such as the Pharisees and the Sadducees. It is clear from these texts that this is an internal Jewish debate. When, according to the Gospels, the Pharisees attacked Jesus because of his behavior, there followed a dispute of a *halachic* [pertaining to Jewish law] nature. Jesus reasons in this context, remaining within the fold of Judaism." ...

Non-Jews Become Christians

Van der Horst says it is difficult to determine where to place the beginning of Christian anti-Semitism. "It varied from location to location. In the Jerusalem Christian community it started much later than in the communities in Asia Minor, Greece, or Rome, or wherever else Christian communities came into being.

"The earliest Christian generation in Jerusalem consisted almost entirely of Jews. These people believed in Jesus as the Messiah, but saw themselves as true Jews. The book of Acts of the Apostles makes it clear that the first Jewish Christians went to the Temple in Jerusalem, attended synagogue services, and wanted to remain Jews. There were tensions with mainstream Jews, who looked askance at the belief that a crucified person was the Messiah. There was, however, no breaking point or even a discussion of excommunicating the Jewish Christians.

"The situation changed slowly in the second generation of Christians. This was directly related to the missionary activities of people like the Apostle Paul and his collaborators. Their vision was that 'salvation,' as they called it, was intended by God not only for the Jewish people but also for others. They began to preach their message to non-Jews outside the Land of Israel as well.

"These earliest missionaries wanted to facilitate the entrance of non-Jews into the growing Christian community. They therefore began to downgrade the Torah (the Pentateuch) and its commandments. Later they started to toy with the idea that, if God wanted non-Jews to be part of the community as well, the commandments of the Torah should be solely for the Jewish members. That gave rise to the first tensions between Jewish and gentile Christians.

"Later on, as is also made quite clear in the New Testament, gentile Christians began to claim that their communities were the true Israel. They asserted that in neglecting many

of the Torah's commandments, they—and not the Jews—
knew what God wanted from His people. The issues of the
centrality and the remaining value and validity of the Torah
were among the first reasons for tensions. Here one sees the
beginnings of a split between Judaism and Christianity.

"With this came the beginning of anti-Jewish sentiments
in Christianity. It was also aggravated by a second factor. In
the same period, perhaps in the second and certainly in the
third generation of Christians—by the end of the first century
of the Common Era—they began to explicitly call Jesus God.
He, as a Jew, had never done so. In the four chronologically
latest books of the New Testament, Jesus is called God, though
only incidentally. These documents are all from around the
turn of the first to the second century: the Gospel of John, the
Epistle of the Hebrews, the Second Epistle of Peter, and the
so-called Epistle of Titus.

"In the Gospel of John it is clear that this is going to be a
breaking point between Jews and Christians. The Gospel's author has Jews saying about Jesus, 'He makes himself equal to
God.' We have to interpret this to mean that it is the Christians who are equating Jesus with God.

"From a Jewish viewpoint this is terrible. Once the Christians began to declare Jesus as equal to God, the core of Jewish monotheism was in danger. The Jewish leaders decided
that they could no longer live under one roof with this group,
which led to the break. The Christians then claimed that the
Jews said they had to throw Jesus' followers out of the synagogue. That is not historical, because it was not said in Jesus'
time but probably later, in the time of the writer of the Gospel of John.

"The Gospel of John is the only one to use the Greek
word *Aposynagogos*. It means 'thrown out of the synagogue'
and reflects the situation around the year 100 CE. Here one
sees for the first time that Judaism and Christianity have split
apart completely. It was probably in more or less the same pe-

riod—which began after the year 70 CE—that the early rabbinical authorities inserted the additional benediction, the *birkat haminim*, into the Amidah [the main daily Jewish prayer].

"This *birkat haminim* consists of a curse of the heretics. Without doubt the Christians at this time held beliefs that contradicted Jewish religious precepts. They were heretics because they no longer lived according to the Torah and they regarded a human being as God. These two major factors caused the definitive split between Judaism and Christianity.

"There were some lesser reasons as well. One was that in the Jewish wars against the Romans in 66 and 132, the Christians did not fight against the Romans. The Jews reproached them for this."...

Anti-Semitism in the Gospels

When asked about the anti-Jewish texts in the Gospel of Matthew, van der Horst answers: "That fits into another picture that is not in itself anti-Semitic. Only in this Gospel's passion narrative of Jesus does one find that Pilate, the Roman governor of Judea, says 'I do not see anything evil in this man.' Pilate then washes his hands as a token of his wish to have nothing to do with Jesus' execution. Pilate's wife says, 'I had a dream about this man. Don't touch him because he is completely innocent.' This text is blatantly unhistorical. Everything we know from other sources tells us that Pilate was thoroughly unscrupulous and ruthless. The idea that he would save a person from capital punishment because he thought him innocent is almost ridiculous.

"Why then does Matthew exculpate [relieve of blame] the Romans from the death of Jesus? The text has to be understood in the context of his time, around the 80s of the first century. In the middle of the 60s CE, under the Emperor Nero, the first persecutions of Christians had begun. There are indications that after that period there were further minor persecutions on a local level. This frightened the Christians.

53

"For political reasons Matthew was keen that his writings should give the Romans the impression that Christians were not a danger to their empire. If a highly positioned person like Pilate says about Jesus 'This man is completely innocent,' it implies that Christianity is not something Romans have to fear. This in turn leads to the story of the Jews supposedly shouting 'Let his blood come over us'—which means, 'We take the responsibility for his death.' Shifting the responsibility for Jesus' death to the Jewish people is at odds with what Matthew says in the earlier parts of his Gospel to the effect that Jesus enjoyed immense popularity with the masses, that is, with the majority of the common Jewish people.

"There is also an isolated case of an anti-Jewish outburst by the Apostle Paul. In one of his letters to the Thessalonians, the Christian community in the Greek town of Thessalonica, he reports that the Jews strongly oppose his preaching. Paul then works himself into a fury and says, 'These Jews killed Jesus and the prophets and for that reason they displease God and are the enemies of all mankind.'

"This is the only text in the New Testament that says the Jews are the enemy of the rest of mankind. This motif derives from pre-Christian pagan anti-Semitism, where it appears many times. It stands in complete opposition to what Paul says at length about the Jewish people in his Epistle to the Romans. In three chapters—9, 10, and 11—Paul paints a far more positive picture of the Jewish people. There is no mention of their being the enemy of humanity; nor is there any in Paul's other letters.

"In his later letter to the Romans, Paul says: 'We Christians should realize that the olive tree is the people of Israel and we are only grafted into this olive tree.' His one case of an anti-Jewish outburst seems to be that of someone who did not always control his emotions."

Van der Horst relates to the often asked question whether the New Testament itself has anti-Semitic elements. "I would

The Roots of Modern Anti-Semitism

Many scholars have urged us to disentangle the history of Catholic-Jewish tensions from the history of modern anti-Semitism, arguing that these two phenomena have different roots and different consequences. The historian Krzysztof Lewalski, for example, distinguishes between "anti-Judaic" beliefs (the theological teachings that distinguish Christianity from Judaism), "anti-Jewish" attitudes (the day-to-day hostilities that came from social and economic conflicts between Jewish and Christian communities), and anti-Semitism *sensu stricto* [in the strict sense] (the distinctly modern ideology of racialized hatred). Others have rejected this differentiation. Most famously, David Kertzer argues that the Church propagated all the major tenets of modern anti-Semitism, thus serving as "antechamber to the Holocaust.". . . If we set aside both the indictments and the apologetics we are left with two points that are hard to dispute: representations of the Jews in Catholic texts (particularly prior to World War I) did indeed differ from the writings of secular, racial anti-Semites; nonetheless it is impossible to completely separate Catholic anti-Semitism from racial anti-Semitism, because religious hatred and secular hatred coexisted in mutually formative ways. Catholic anti-Semitism would not have taken the shape it did had racialist ideas not been such a key component of European culture at the time, and secular anti-Semitism could not have gained so much support had it not shared a lot of common ground with Christianity.

Brian Porter-Szücs,
Faith and Fatherland, *2011.*

say yes, but again only in the chronologically latest documents. The clearest instance is that of the Gospel of John. There one sees that the split between Christians and Jews has occurred. It has happened recently and that is also why the language is so vehement. The anti-Jewish sentiment permeates the whole book, and it contains the most anti-Semitic verse in the New Testament.

"The author has Jesus distance himself completely from the Jewish people. He lets him speak about the Jews, their laws and festivals, as if he himself is no longer one of them. Worst of all, in a dispute between Jesus and the Jewish leaders, John has him say: 'You have the devil as your father.' In later Christian literature, that expression is picked up. This fatal short remark has had lethal consequences over two millennia. It cost tens of thousands of Jewish lives in later history, especially in the Middle Ages. This verse was taken by Christian Jew-haters as a license to murder Jews. These murderers thought: 'If Jesus says that Jews have the devil as their father, we should eradicate them as best as we can.'

"All New Testament scholars agree that Jesus did not say what John puts into his mouth, but that it is the position of the Gospel's author. When one religious group breaks away from its mother religion, it has to create its own new identity. The sociology of religion teaches us that, in its first phase, the new group always begins to attack the old religion as fiercely as it can and to demonize it. The most effective demonization is calling the Jews 'children of the devil' and having Jesus, the most important person in the new religion, say this himself.

"I once argued before an audience of Christian ministers that if we were to confront John with the consequences of what he wrote, he would deeply apologize and say, 'Please, delete it from my Gospel.' Until the present day these words have their influence, because the average Bible reader cannot contextualize them in the first century when they were written. The Gospel of John unfortunately is also one of the most popular books in Christianity." . . .

A Global Christian Church

Van der Horst explains that by the end of the first century, all or most of the documents that would form the New Testament had been written, but had not yet been canonized. "Deciding what belonged to the Christian canon took several centuries. Only by the end of the second century do we find for the first time a list of books of the New Testament. Several documents that nowadays are part of it were not yet included.

"It would take two more centuries before there was a complete New Testament. Until then there were disagreements about what was authoritative between, for instance, the communities in Asia Minor, Syria, and Egypt. One needed an overarching organization to unify the texts. The definitive canon of the New Testament as we now know it dates from the fourth century.

"Predominantly gentile Christianity slowly began to organize into what one would call a global church. Quite soon, the anti-Jewish sentiments and doctrines became part and parcel of the official doctrine of the mainline church. This occurred from the middle of the second century onward. In Sardis in western Turkey, Bishop Melito, in his so-called Peri Pascha [Paschal, that is, Easter, sermon], says many negative things about the Jews and accuses them of having killed Jesus. Because Jesus is now clearly considered a God, the motif of deicide becomes one of the main elements in the anti-Jewish doctrines of the church.

"In Sardis there was a major synagogue, the ruins of which exist till today. The Jewish community there went on to flourish so much that even by the end of antiquity, or the early Middle Ages, i.e. the sixth and seventh centuries, this synagogue was still the largest religious building in town, larger than the main church.

"Gradually the motif of Jews being Christ-killers assumed a major role in the church's anti-Jewish preaching. This is still very much alive in our day. Only many years after the Holocaust has the accusation that the Jews are responsible for the death of Jesus been officially rescinded by mainstream Protestantism and the Roman Catholic Church. It is, however, still adhered to by many of their followers.

"The motif of deicide committed by Jews is very much alive in other major churches, especially Orthodox ones such as the Russian, Greek, Serbian, and Bulgarian Orthodox Churches. The poisonous combination of the Jews being both guilty of deicide and children of the devil flourishes there. The two elements reinforce each other."

"Among the church fathers, some are quite mild in their position toward Judaism while others are fiercely hostile. John Chrysostom, one of the best-known church fathers, is one of the most anti-Jewish.

"This bishop of Antioch, Syria, lived in the second half of the fourth and the beginning of the fifth century. His name means 'man with the golden mouth,' but much venom came from this mouth. He is not the first, but certainly the most outspoken, church father who combined horrific Christian anti-Jewish elements derived from the New Testament with originally pagan ones.

"John Chrysostom's most notorious writings are a series of long anti-Jewish sermons, which he delivered in the main church of Antioch in 386 and 387 CE. They belong to the worst Christian anti-Semitic documents in antiquity. Besides calling the Jews 'Christ-killers'—claiming they killed the person who was sent to them by God to save them in the Final Judgment—and 'children of the devil,' he also adopted various anti-Jewish clichés from pre-Christian pagan antiquity. These include motifs such as the Jews as haters of the rest of humanity and as nonbelievers in any god whatsoever.

"John Chrysostom and others could also reach back to the one statement where the Apostle Paul said the Jews were enemies of mankind. Through John Chrysostom these themes began to be integrated into the anti-Jewish discourse of Christianity. His anti-Jewish sermons have since become very influential." . . .

Jewish Anti-Christian Discourse

"If one reviews the writings of the church fathers from the second to the sixth centuries, almost all are anti-Jewish. This discourse has become part and parcel of the doctrine of mainstream Christianity. This may be due partly to the anti-Christian discourse that Jews developed as a reaction to the attacks on them by Christians.

"In the second century one already hears from church fathers that Jews are spreading the story that Jesus was not born of a virgin, that his father was not God or a holy spirit, and even that Joseph, Mary's husband, was not his father. The story claimed that Jesus was the child of Mary and a Roman soldier called Panthera and thus that she was an adulteress.

"This is confirmed by Jewish sources. For instance, another text from the sixth or seventh century, the so-called *Toldot Yeshu* [History of Jesus], elaborates on this story. Besides saying that Jesus is the son of a Roman soldier, it claims that his healing miracles were magic tricks learned in Egypt with the purpose of destroying the Torah. We only know of some cases of such anti-Christian statements, but they are relatively well anchored in historical facts and are also found in the Talmud.

"On some occasions Jews participated with the Romans in the persecution of Christians, so they were not only victims. Jews struck back on a much more limited scale than the church, which gradually achieved its position of power after the first Christian emperor Constantine allowed Christianity to exist in the Roman Empire in 313.

"While the Jews did not remain silent, their reactions had to be careful and limited, especially after the Roman Empire had officially become Christian at the end of the fourth century. Around 390 CE, the Emperor Theodosius I decreed that Christianity was the only acceptable religion. This did not mean that from then onward all people in the Roman Empire became Christians. There was fierce opposition, especially from the aristocrats who clung to their Roman or Greek religions. The Jews were not the church's main target in that period as it still had to fight with the old pagans. That took one to two more centuries.

"The situation concerning the Jews more or less stabilized in the lifetime of the best-known church father, Augustine, who lived in Hippo in today's Tunisia in the second half of the fourth and the beginning of the fifth century. He said with great authority that the Jews were a damned people but should not be persecuted and killed. They should be kept alive as witnesses that Christianity was right.

"Augustine did not want to convert Jews by force. Such forced conversion remained rare in antiquity. The first major case occurred around 630 CE in the Byzantine Empire, when the Emperor Heraclius decreed that all Jews there must be baptized and converted to Christianity. We know from historical sources that this decree was carried out in some places. Elsewhere, however, the authorities did nothing. This case occurred in the period when Islam was on the rise and only a few years before Muslims captured Jerusalem."

Van der Horst concludes: "Over the centuries many discriminatory measures have been taken in Christian environments against Jews. The infrastructure for this was laid in the early history of Christianity, albeit not in the time of Jesus' life or immediately thereafter."

> *"Pope Pius XII could not collaborate with the Nazis, the Soviets or any other regime founded upon ideals alien to those of his Church. Instead, . . . he had to oppose them."*

The Christian Church Opposed the Social Darwinism That Fed Nazi Anti-Semitism

Harry Schnitker

Harry Schnitker is the senior supervisor of ecclesiastical history at Maryvale Ecclesiastical Institute for Religious Sciences in Birmingham, England. In the following viewpoint, he argues that the Catholic Church and the Christian gospels were radically opposed to the philosophy of social Darwinism. This philosophy held that certain human races were superior to others and that only the fittest races should survive. Schnitker asserts that it was used by the Nazis to justify the Holocaust. Schnitker acknowledges that there was also a Christian tradition of anti-Semitism.

Nonetheless, he argues that the pope and the Catholic Church steadfastly opposed the Nazi's brand of Jewish hatred and its genocidal results.

As you read, consider the following questions:

1. According to Schnitker, who coined the phrase "survival of the fittest," and what political philosophy did the coiner support?

2. What currents does the author say collided and merged with social Darwinism, and what effect did this have?

3. What did the pope say about eugenic euthanasia, according to Schnitker?

Pope Pius XII [played several key roles] during the Second World War. Of these, his relationship with the Jews and the Germans, the two peoples central to almost every narrative of the war, are the most essential. The Holy Father's experience of Marxism and his radical denunciation of the philosophy [are well known]. What is rarely mentioned, however, is that Fascism and Nazism and Communism—and, indeed, radical free market capitalism—share a common source: Social Darwinism.

The Survival of the Fittest

In essence, Social Darwinism is the transfer of Charles Darwin's evolutionary ideas onto the field of human society. It was very popular during the later nineteenth century, particularly in Britain and the United States, and has retained its nefarious hold on several political movements to this day. Most would not recognize the label, which is usually, but correctly, applied to them by their opponents. Chief amongst these is the Catholic Church.

To understand why Social Darwinism has been such a problem for the Church, one has to examine its basic tenets,

Charles Darwin and Adolf Hitler

In her *New York Times* bestselling book *The Age of American Unreason*, Susan Jacoby refers to social Darwinism as "a form of ideologically driven pseudoscience intended to rationalize the Gilded Age's excesses of wealth and poverty. The new pseudoscience of social Darwinism, like the ancient pseudoscience of astrology and alchemy, used scientific language to mask an essentially unscientific essence." Yes, social Darwinism is a pseudoscience. But how does Jacoby distance herself so quickly from an "ideologically driven pseudoscience" when in fact social Darwinism is perfectly suitable with Darwinian principles?...

The leading intellectuals who promoted social Darwinism took Darwinian principles to their logical conclusions. John D. Rockefeller, William Graham Sumner, and others understood Darwin's natural selection perfectly well, and applied it to the "inferior" races, the "mentally" retarded, and other undesirables. In fact, as the Nazi historian Richard Weikari shows in his work *From Darwin to Hitler: Evolutionary Ethics, Eugenics, and Racism in Nazi Germany*, social Darwinism was one of the underlying ideologies that drove the Nazi regime into madness. Hitler declared in *Mein Kampf*: "Whoever is not bodily [or] spiritually healthy and worthy, shall not have the right to pass on his suffering in the body of his children."

Jonas E. Alexis,
Christianity's Dangerous Idea, *2010.*

and compare these with the principles of our Faith as taught by Jesus, the Apostles and their successors [i.e., Roman Catholic bishops]. When the earliest social commentators began to read Darwin, what struck them most was the notion of the survival of the fittest. This was, even then, a crude reading of Darwin's theory of evolution. Darwin suggested that species survive because they develop a set of tools to cope with their environment and their competitors. This does not suggest a survival of the fittest at all; it merely suggests that species adapt to survive.

Applied to human society, this faulty reading became in the first place a pseudo-scientific justification for the unrestrained free market and capitalism. It appeared that the natural world justified the failure to protect the weak, and, in the crude notion of the Social Darwinists, this allowed mankind to follow its basic instinct. The notion of the 'survival of the fittest' was coined, not by Darwin, but by Herbert Spencer (1820–1903), in his *Principles of Biology* of 1864. Spencer would later write another seminal work of Capitalist philosophy, *The Man versus the State*, in which all forms of state intervention on behalf of the weakest was denounced.

An even more violent attack on the sanctity of human beings came from the pen of another British thinker, Francis Galton (1822–1911). Galton has been called the father of modern eugenics [the idea that humanity should genetically improve itself, sometimes by preventing those considered racially and mentally inferior from breeding], and was an extremely intelligent man, who, unfortunately, channeled his intelligence into thinking about Social Darwinism. Convinced that nature was more important than nurture—he coined the phrase—Galton devised elaborate notions of racial and class superiority. To ensure that the human race would develop its full potential, Galton believed that 'breeding programs' were in order for the fittest and the hereditary strongest. He did not develop the logical counterpart to his idea, but that was easy enough for his subsequent followers.

Racial Anti-Semitism

These trends merged with two other currents in Europe. The first was an ancient one: Anti-Semitism. The hatred of Jews was nothing new in nineteenth- and twentieth-century Europe. It has deep roots, which fed popular dislike of strangers during the Middle Ages, and which found erroneous justification in the 'fact' that the Jews had killed Jesus. Of course, the Jews had not done so, but the Romans, but this did not stop the hatred. Frequently, the Church, or members of the Church, encouraged this Anti-Semitism, and its critics are correct in stating that the extermination camps have some Christian roots. Popes often went out of their way to protect Europe's Jews, but that did not stop local bishops. Despicable though this religious Anti-Semitism was, it has to be distinguished from the racial Anti-Semitism that was fed by Social Darwinism. This had begun to divide the single human race, all created in God's image, into fictitious 'races,' deploying all the tricks of acceptable scientific techniques, without pausing to think that these may not be acceptable to a later age. The Jews featured rather lowly in this order of races, and this found a ready audience amongst the disenfranchised of Europe, including, in Vienna, one Adolph Hitler. Combined with eugenics as a means of achieving the perfect human race, it would prove to be a lethal notion.

The second important current that collided and merged with Social Darwinism was nationalism. Increasingly, Europeans saw their nation as the essence of their identity, at the expense of everything else. It was an attitude that reduced the value of human life to its usefulness for its country. Young men died for their country, and if they refused to do so, were executed or imprisoned. A whole industry sprang up to promote the hatred and fear of those in other countries. In many instances, this coincided with a growing ethnic awareness. It became more important to be German than to live under the rule of a particular ruler, to pick just one example.

Again Social Darwinism and the idea of specific human 'races' merged with these nationalist tendencies. The idea grew that a race should have its own national state, but this ignored the patchwork of ethnicities that marked much of Europe. Eugenics came to be seen as a logical solution to the problem, as did ethnic cleansing. All ideologies that dominated Europe between 1918 and 1939 were, to some extent, indebted to Social Darwinism. The free market democracies of Britain and France had their system underpinned by its theories, which allowed [then British chancellor of the exchequer, similar to secretary of the treasury] Winston Churchill to wage war on striking miners—they undermined the strength of the country and challenged those 'born to govern'.

In Italy and Spain, as well as in many eastern European countries, it created the atmosphere in which a strongman could govern, on behalf of the nation, of course. In the Soviet Union it allowed the fullest implementation of [Joseph] Stalin's horrors as the natural conclusion of the struggle for control between the weaker, bourgeois class and the virility of the working classes. I am not arguing here, as some historians have done, that Social Darwinism is the sole source of all the ideologies with which Pope Pius XII was confronted when he ascended St. Peter's throne in 1939. However, the impact of the various strains of Social Darwinism is unmistakable.

The Gospel and the Nazis

That any ideology influenced by this way of thinking would find the Catholic Church in its way hardly needs explanation. The notion that it is natural for mankind to trample the weakest underfoot, and the idea that somehow we ought to 'improve' on God's plan through eugenics are, simply, incompatible with the values of the Gospel. Pope Pius XII could not collaborate with the Nazis, the Soviets or any other regime founded upon ideals alien to those of his Church. Instead, he found he had to oppose them, as had all his predecessors since the middle of the nineteenth century. The Holy Father repeated time and again the simple statement of the Church:

God created mankind in His own image, and every human is part of one family, and has enormous value.

In December 1940, he published his single strongest condemnation of eugenics. Posing the question whether euthanasia was ever lawful, his answer was "No, because it is contrary to the natural law and the divine precept". This 'no' applied to the disabled as well as those of different ethnicities—Jews, Gypsies et al.—and those whose sexuality differed from the prevailing norm, such as homosexuals. Direct interference in God's plan, in accordance with Social Darwinist thinking was, simply, anti-Catholic. Of course, we have to look no further than the famous Encyclical which [as Cardinal] Pacelli [Pius XII] wrote for his predecessor, Pius XI, *Mit Brennender Sorge* [*With Burning Concern*]:

> In the furrows, where We tried to sow the seed of a sincere peace, other men—the "enemy" of Holy Scripture—oversowed the cockle [burr] of distrust, unrest, hatred, defamation, of a determined hostility overt or veiled, fed from many sources and wielding many tools, against Christ and His Church.

The Nazis were not 'just' the enemy of the Church, they were the enemy of 'Holy Scripture'. There were many reasons for this, but the main one lay in the field of their wholesale embrace of the ideologies of Social Darwinism. One simply cannot understand the role of Pope Pius XII during the Second World War without understanding this fact, and without realizing that it informed the Pontiff's every reaction against the regime in Berlin.

> "[Palestinian militant group] Hamas' views on Islamic Jew hatred are entirely concordant with those of the most authoritative religious educational institution within Sunni Islam."

Anti-Semitism in the Islamic World Has Deep Religious Roots

Andrew Bostom, as told to Mark Tapson

Andrew Bostom is an associate professor of medicine at Brown University in Providence, Rhode Island, and the author of The Legacy of Islamic Antisemitism; *Mark Tapson writes on politics and culture for* Acculturated, FrontPage, PJ Media, *and other outlets. In the following viewpoint taken from Tapson's interview of Bostom, Bostom argues that anti-Semitism has long been a part of Muslim teaching. As evidence, he points to anti-Semitic passages in the Koran and other Muslim texts and to the treatment of Jews and other non-Muslims in past Muslim-governed areas. He concludes that traditional Muslim anti-Semitic rhetoric is still used by Muslims today and that anti-Semitism is intertwined with Islam.*

As you read, consider the following questions:

1. What does Bostom say inspired his decision to study Islam?

2. What traditional restrictions on non-Muslims by Muslim governments does Bostom list?

3. What are some examples of Muslim violence against Jews since 1900 that Bostom discusses?

In the wake of the farcically mislabeled "Arab Spring" [a wave of revolutions in Arab nations beginning in December 2010], we are witnessing a swelling tide of Jew-hatred emanating from the triumphant Islamists throughout the Middle East who don't even bother to conceal it. And why should they? Our own willfully blind and/or complicit media downplay it or ignore it altogether.

Some argue that what is mistaken for contemporary Islamic anti-Semitism is just a reaction to Israel's "occupation" and "genocidal oppression" of the Palestinians. Or that it is not intrinsic to Islam but derives from the influence of Nazism. Or that it is a perversion of Islam on the part of a tiny minority of extremists. What are the true roots of Islamic Jew-hatred?

Andrew Bostom, M.D., M.S., has documented the answer. An Associate Professor of Medicine at Rhode Island Hospital, the major teaching affiliate of Brown University Medical School, he is the author of two essential, extraordinary, and meticulously documented works of scholarship, *The Legacy of Jihad* and *The Legacy of Islamic Antisemitism*, and of the upcoming *Sharia versus Freedom* (with a foreword by the incomparable Andrew C. McCarthy). He has published articles and commentary on Islam here on *FrontPage* and in the *Washington Times, National Review Online, Revue Politique, American Thinker*, and elsewhere in print and online. . . .

Mark Tapson: *Dr. Bostom, what inspired you as a scholar to focus on Islam?*

Andrew Bostom: It's pretty straightforward. The stimulus was 9/11/2001. Until then I was simply a medical academic at Rhode Island Hospital (the major teaching hospital of The Warren Alpert Medical School of Brown University), and an average citizen trying to keep abreast of world events. I am not particularly religious as a Jew though I certainly support the state of Israel. But I grew up in New York, living in Queens most of my life, and I went to medical school in Brooklyn. My wife and I still have family in New York City, so the day of 9/11/2001 itself was traumatic, trying to make sure everyone was OK. A colleague's wife was in the second tower. She was very lucky, barely getting out before it collapsed.

On the way home I grabbed a book by Karen Armstrong about Islam. I was reading it and commenting to my wife that it just didn't seem to jibe. (I learned later that Armstrong is a notorious apologist.) As I read it out loud my wife was just laughing. I didn't find it particularly funny. Nor the news reports over the next days that were transparently apologetic. And I was alarmed at stories that appeared in the *New York Times* (and other New York area newspapers) about an Egyptian Imam who was preaching at a large Mosque in Manhattan, and spreading conspiracy theories about Jews leaving the World Trade Center in advance of the attacks, due to their "prior knowledge."

So I started reading independently. A small book by Yossef Bodansky, a terrorism expert, discussed Islamic anti-semitism as a political instrument, and referenced the work of Bat Ye'or on the dhimmi [non-Muslim citizens of an Islamic state]. I got that book by Bat Ye'or, and everything else she has written in English—all her books, essays, and published lectures. I met Bat Ye'or after a correspondence with [Mideast expert] Daniel Pipes, and brought her to Brown University to give a guest lecture. She became a very close mentor, and introduced me to Ibn Warraq [the pen name of an author well-known for his criticism of Islam] and that's how things started. I had begun writing short essays within a year of 9/11. Ibn Warraq resided with us in 2003, for a time, and he encouraged me to consider a book project. I was increasingly interested in the Jihad and it was with Warraq's support that I put that first book, *The Legacy of Jihad*, together.

Sacralized Hatred

What do you say to the common defense that Islam preaches tolerance toward Christians and Jews—"the people of the book"— and that Jew-hatred is not inherent within it?

Although often invoked, these apologetic canards [misleading fabrications] are diametrically opposed to Islamic doctrine and the sad, if predictable historical realities this sacralized hatred has engendered, what has always been the nature of the system of governance imposed upon indigenous non-Muslims conquered by Islam's timeless, institutionalized jihad wars.

In his seminal *The Laws of Islamic Governance*, al-Mawardi (d. 1058)—a renowned jurist of Baghdad—examined the regulations pertaining to the lands and infidel populations subjugated by jihad. This is the origin of the system of dhimmitude. The native infidel "dhimmi" (which derives from both the word for "pact" and also "guilt"—guilty of religious errors) population had to recognize Islamic ownership of their land, submit to Islamic law, and accept payment of the Koranic poll tax (jizya, the tax paid in lieu of being slain) based on Koran 9:29. Al-Mawardi notes: "The enemy makes a payment in return for peace and reconciliation. . . . Reconciliation and security last as long as the payment is made. If the payment ceases, then the jihad resumes." A treaty of reconciliation may be renewable, but must not exceed 10 years.

This same basic formulation was reiterated during a January 8, 1998, interview by Muslim Brotherhood "Spiritual

Guide," and immensely popular Al-Jazeera [an Arabic-language network] television personality Yusuf al-Qaradawi, confirming how jihad continues to regulate the relations between Muslims and non-Muslims to this day. The "contract of the jizya," or "dhimma," encompassed other obligatory and recommended obligations for the conquered non-Muslim "dhimmi" peoples. Collectively, these "obligations" formed the discriminatory system of dhimmitude imposed upon non-Muslims—Jews and Christians, as well as Zoroastrians, Hindus, and Buddhists—subjugated by jihad. Some of the more salient features of dhimmitude include:

- The prohibition of arms for the vanquished dhimmis

- The prohibition of church bells

- Restrictions concerning the building and restoration of churches, synagogues, and temples

- Inequality between Muslims and non-Muslims with regard to taxes and penal law

- The refusal of dhimmi testimony by Muslim courts

- A requirement that Jews, Christians, and other non-Muslims, including Zoroastrians and Hindus, wear special clothes

- The overall humiliation and abasement of non-Muslims

Institutionalized Discrimination

It is important to note that these regulations and attitudes were institutionalized as permanent features of the sacred Islamic law, or Sharia. The writings of the much lionized Sufi theologian and jurist al-Ghazali (d. 1111) highlight how the institution of dhimmitude was simply a normative and prominent feature of the Sharia:

> The dhimmi is obliged not to mention Allah or His Apostle. . . . Jews, Christians, and Majians must pay the

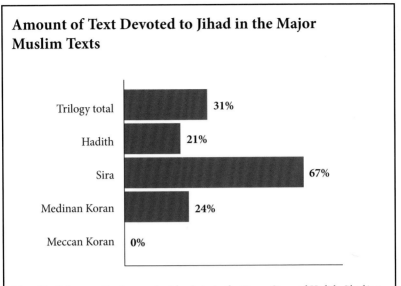

Amount of Text Devoted to Jihad in the Major Muslim Texts

Note: The Trilogy are the three major Islamic texts: the Koran, Sira, and Hadith. *Jihad* is a term for "holy war."

TAKEN FROM: Bill Warner, "Islam and the Egyptian Political Future," *The American Thinker*, February 9, 2011.

jizya. . . . On offering up the jizya, the dhimmi must hang his head while the official takes hold of his beard and hits [the dhimmi] on the protruberant bone beneath his ear [i.e., the jaw]. . . . They are not permitted to ostentatiously display their wine or church bells. . . . Their houses may not be higher than the Muslim's, no matter how low that is. The dhimmi may not ride an elegant horse or mule; he may ride a donkey only if the saddle-work is of wood. He may not walk on the good part of the road. They [the dhimmis] have to wear [an identifying] patch [on their clothing], even women, and even in the [public] baths. . . . [Dhimmis] must hold their tongue.

The practical consequences of such a discriminatory system were summarized by the great historian of Muslim and non-Muslim (especially Jewish) relations during classical Islam, S.D. Goitein, in 1970:

Taxation [by the Muslim government] was merciless, and a very large section of the population must have lived permanently at the starvation level. From many Geniza letters [a trove of Oriental Jewish correspondence et al., particularly from the Middle Ages, discovered in Egypt] one gets the impression that the poor were concerned more with getting money for the payment of their taxes than for food and clothing, for failure of payment usually induced cruel punishment. . . . The Muslim state was quite the opposite of the ideals . . . embedded in the constitution of the United States. An Islamic state was part of or coincided with dar al-Islam, the House of Islam. Its treasury was . . . the money of the Muslims. Christians and Jews were not citizens of the state, not even second-class citizens. They were outsiders under the protection of the Muslim state, a status characterized by the term *dhimma*. . . . They were also exposed to a great number of discriminatory and humiliating laws. . . . As it lies in the very nature of such restrictions, soon additional humiliations were added, and before the second century of Islam was out, a complete body of legislation in this matter was in existence. . . . In times and places in which they became too oppressive they led to the dwindling or even complete extinction of the minorities.

Important scholars of Islamic Antisemitism—from Hartwig Hirschfeld in the mid-1880s, Georges Vajda in the late 1930s, S.D. Goitein in 1971, and Haggai Ben-Shammai in 1988—have demonstrated, collectively, all of the following:

- Clear historical evidence of specific Islamic antisemitism, from the Geniza record of the high Middle Ages—including the coinage of a unique Hebrew word to characterize such Muslim Jew hatred, *sinuth*—published in full by Goitein as of 1971

- The content of foundational Muslim sources detailing the sacralized rationale for Islam's anti-Jewish bigotry, including Hartwig Hirschfeld's mid-1880s essay series on Muhammad's subjugation of the Jews of Medina, based upon the earliest pious Muslim biographies of Muhammad

- George Vajda's elegant, comprehensive 1937 analysis focusing primarily on the hadith (the putative words and deeds of the Muslim prophet Muhammad, as recorded by his earliest pious Muslim companions)

- Haggai Ben-Shammai's concise 1988 study of key examples of Jew-hatred in the Koran and Koranic exegesis

For example, Koran 3:112 is featured before the preamble to [militant Islamic Palestinian group] Hamas' foundational Covenant—it is literally part of the very first statement of the document. Here is the standard . . . translation of 3:112:

Abasement shall be pitched on them, wherever they are come upon, except they be in a bond of God, and a bond of the people; they will be laden with the burden of God's anger, and poverty shall be pitched on them; that, because they disbelieved in God's signs, and slew the Prophets without right; that, for that they acted rebelliously and were transgressors.

In classical and modern Koranic exegeses by seminal, authoritative Islamic theologians this central motif is coupled to Koranic verses 5:60, and 5:78, which describe the Jews transformation into apes and pigs, or simply apes, having been ". . . cursed by the tongue of David, and Jesus, Mary's son." Muhammad himself—Islam's founding prophet—repeats this Koranic curse in a canonical hadith, "He [Muhammad] then recited the verse: '. . . curses were pronounced on those among the children of Israel who rejected Faith, by the tongue of David and of Jesus the son of Mary.'" And the related verse, 5:64, accuses the Jews—as Palestinian Authority President Mahmoud Abbas did in a January 2007 speech, citing Koran 5:64—of being "spreaders of war and corruption," a sort of ancient Koranic antecedent of *The Protocols of the Elders of Zion* [an infamous anti-Semitic book from 1903].

Jews as Murderers and the Anti-Christ

The Koranic curse upon the Jews for (primarily) rejecting, even slaying Allah's prophets, including Isa, the Muslim Jesus (or at least his "body double"), is updated with perfect thematic logic in the canonical hadith: following the Muslims' initial conquest of the Jewish farming oasis of Khaybar, one of the vanquished Jewesses reportedly served Muhammad poisoned mutton (or goat), which resulted, ultimately, in his protracted, agonizing death. And Ibn Saad's sira account—the sira being the earliest pious Muslim biographies of Muhammad—maintains that Muhammad's poisoning resulted from a well-coordinated Jewish conspiracy.

As characterized in the hadith, Muslim eschatology [the theology of the end of the world] highlights the Jews' supreme hostility to Islam. Jews are described as adherents of the Dajjâl—the Muslim equivalent of the Anti-Christ—or according to another tradition, the Dajjâl is himself Jewish. At his appearance, other traditions maintain that the Dajjâl will be accompanied by 70,000 Jews from Isfahan, or Jerusalem, wrapped in their robes, and armed with polished sabers, their heads covered with a sort of veil. When the Dajjâl is defeated, his Jewish companions will be slaughtered—everything will deliver them up except for the so-called gharkad tree, as per the canonical hadith included in the 1988 Hamas Covenant. This hadith is cited in the Covenant as a sacralized, obligatory call for a Muslim genocide of the Jews:

> ... the Islamic Resistance Movement aspires to realize the promise of Allah, no matter how long it takes. The Prophet, Allah's prayer and peace be upon him, says: "The hour of judgment shall not come until the Muslims fight the Jews and kill them, so that the Jews hide behind trees and stones, and each tree and stone will say: 'Oh Muslim, oh servant of

Allah, there is a Jew behind me, come and kill him,' except for the Gharqad tree, for it is the tree of the Jews."

Moreover, findings reported by the politically left Israel Foundation, July 15, 2011, from an "intensive, face-to-face survey in Arabic of 1,010 Palestinian adults in the West Bank and the Gaza Strip" revealed that 73% of this representative statistical sample of Palestinians surveyed agree with the dictates of the annihilationist canonical hadith quoted in the Hamas Covenant.

Unfortunately, Hamas' views on Islamic Jew hatred, are entirely concordant with those of the most authoritative religious educational institution within Sunni Islam [the largest Islamic denomination] for over 1,000 years, since the late 10th century—Al Azhar University, in Cairo, Egypt. Consider a fatwa [a ruling on Islamic law by an Islamic scholar] written January 5, 1956, by then Grand Mufti of Egypt, Sheikh Hasan Ma'moun, and signed by the leading members of the Fatwa Committee of Al Azhar, and the major representatives of all four Sunni Islamic schools of jurisprudence. This ruling elaborated the following key initial point: that all of historical Palestine—modern Jordan, Israel, and the disputed territories of Judea and Samaria, as well as Gaza—having been conquered by jihad, was a permanent possession of the global Muslim umma (community), "fay territory"—booty or spoils—to be governed eternally by Islamic Law. The January, 1956 Al Azhar fatwa's language and arguments are indistinguishable from those employed by Hamas (in its Covenant), revealing the same conjoined motivations of jihad, and conspiratorial Islamic Jew hatred:

> Muslims cannot conclude peace with those Jews who have usurped the territory of Palestine and attacked its people and their property in any manner which allows the Jews to continue as a state in that sacred Muslim territory.
>
> [As] Jews have taken a part of Palestine and there established their non-Islamic government and have also evacu-

ated from that part most of its Muslim inhabitants . . . Jihad
. . . to restore the country to its people . . . is the duty of all
Muslims, not just those who can undertake it. And since all
Islamic countries constitute the abode of every Muslim, the
Jihad is imperative for both the Muslims inhabiting the territory attacked, and Muslims everywhere else because even
though some sections have not been attacked directly, the
attack nevertheless took place on a part of the Muslim territory which is a legitimate residence for any Muslim.

*Everyone knows that from the early days of Islam to the present
day the Jews have been plotting against Islam and Muslims
and the Islamic homeland.* They do not propose to be content with the attack they made on Palestine and Al Aqsa
Mosque, but they plan for the possession of all Islamic territories from the Nile to the Euphrates [i.e., Egypt to Iraq].

Modern Muslim Antisemitism

The continual, monotonous invocation by Al Azhar clerics of
such jihadist and antisemitic motifs from the Koran (or other
foundational Muslim texts) is entirely consistent with the
published writings and statements of the late Sheikh Muhammad Sayyid Tantawi—Grand Imam of this pre-eminent Islamic religious institution from 1996, till his death in March
2010.

My book *The Legacy of Islamic Antisemitism* includes extensive first-time English translations of Tantawi's academic
magnum opus, *Jews in the Koran and the Traditions*. Tantawi
wrote these words rationalizing Muslim Jew-hatred, in his 700
page treatise:

[The] Koran describes the Jews with their own particular
degenerate characteristics, i.e. killing the prophets of Allah
[Koran 2:61/3:112], corrupting His words by putting them
in the wrong places, consuming the people's wealth frivo-
lously, refusal to distance themselves from the evil they do,
and other ugly characteristics caused by their deep-rooted

lasciviousness. . . . Only a minority of the Jews keep their word. . . .[A]ll Jews are not the same. The good ones become Muslims [Koran 3:113], the bad ones do not.

Tantawi was apparently rewarded for this scholarly effort by being named Grand Imam of Al-Azhar University, a position he held for 14-years. These were the expressed, "carefully researched" views on Jews held by the nearest Muslim equivalent to a Pope—the head of the most prestigious center of Muslim learning in Sunni Islam, which represents some 85 to 90% of the world's Muslims. And Sheikh Tantawi never mollified such hatemongering beliefs after becoming the Grand Imam of Al-Azhar as his statements on "dialogue" (January 1998) with Jews, the Jews as "enemies of Allah, descendants of apes and pigs" (April 2002), and the legitimacy of homicide bombing of Jews (April 2002) make clear.

Here is but a very incomplete sampling of barely known pogroms [systematic persecutions] and mass murderous violence against Jews living under Islamic rule, across space and time, all resulting from the combined effects of jihadism, general anti-dhimmi, and/or specifically Antisemitic motifs in Islam: 6,000 Jews massacred in Fez in 1033; hundreds of Jews slaughtered in Muslim Cordoba between 1010 and 1015; 4,000 Jews killed in Muslim riots in Grenada in 1066, wiping out the entire community; the Berber Muslim Almohad depredations of Jews (and Christians) in Spain and North Africa between 1130 and 1232, which killed tens of thousands, while forcibly converting thousands more, and subjecting the forced Jewish converts to Islam to a Muslim Inquisition; the 1291 pogroms in Baghdad and its environs, which killed (at least) hundreds of Jews; the 1465 pogrom against the Jews of Fez; the late 15th century pogrom against the Jews of the Southern Moroccan oasis town of Touat; the 1679 pogroms against, and then expulsion of 10,000 Jews from Sanaa, Yemen to the unlivable, hot and dry Plain of Tihama, from which only 1,000 returned alive, in 1680, 90% having died from exposure; recurring Muslim anti-Jewish violences—including pogroms and forced conversions—throughout the 17th, 18th and 19th centuries, which rendered areas of Iran (for example, Tabriz) *Judenrein* [a Nazi term meaning "empty of Jews"]; the 1834 pogrom in Safed where raging Muslim mobs killed and grievously wounded hundreds of Jews; the 1888 massacres of Jews in Isfahan and Shiraz, Iran; the 1910 pogrom in Shiraz; the pillage and destruction of the Casablanca, Morocco ghetto in 1907; the pillage of the ghetto of Fez Morocco in 1912; the government sanctioned anti-Jewish pogroms by Muslims in Turkish Eastern Thrace during June–July, 1934 which ethnically cleansed at least 3000 Jews; and the series of pogroms, expropriations, and finally mass expulsions of some 900,000 Jews from Arab Muslim nations, beginning in 1941 in Baghdad (the murderous "Farhud," during which 600 Jews were murdered, and at least 12,000 pillaged)—eventually involving cities and towns in Egypt, Morocco, Libya, Syria, Aden, Bahrain, and culminating in 1967 in Tunisia—that accompanied the planning and creation of a Jewish state, Israel, on a portion of the Jews' ancestral homeland.

> *"When Israel does something terrible, anti-Israeli sentiments understandably rise."*

Anti-Semitism in the Islamic World Is Linked to Israeli Actions

Yossi Gurvitz

Yossi Gurvitz is a journalist, blogger, and photographer who has written for Israeli publications including Calcalist *and the* Nana *portal. In the following viewpoint, he argues that Muslim anti-Semitism is linked to Israeli actions. He acknowledges that Muslim traditions include anti-Semitic elements but says that these are less prevalent than the anti-Semitism in Christianity. He argues that Muslim anti-Semitism really became a powerful force only as Zionism and the effort to establish Israel gained momentum. He says that Israel's self-identity as a Jewish state that speaks for all Jews everywhere has pushed those, such as Muslims, who disagree with Israeli policy to turn their hatred against Jews.*

As you read, consider the following questions:

1. What does Gurvitz identify as the first semipublic failure of Israeli intelligence services?

2. What does the author say was supposed to have happened during the "golden age of Andalus"?

3. Which ancient Jewish communities does Gurvitz say were broken as a reaction to Zionism?

The scandal *du jour* is the fact that the US ambassador to Belgium, Howard Gutman, told a Jewish conference last week [November–December 2011] that Islamic anti-Semitism is the result of Israel's treatment of the Palestinians. This common sense statement caused a hue and cry, and it became the biggest news to come out of the land of chocolate and pederasts, drowning even the fact it finally managed to cobble together a government. The grand inquisitor of all things anti-Semitic, the man who turned his Jewishness into his trade, Jeffrey Goldberg, wrote acerbically that "Here is a simple formula that could have saved Gutman from his stupid mistake: Jews do not cause anti-Semitism; blacks do not cause racism; gays do not cause homophobia. Hatred is a mental and spiritual illness, not a political position."

If only things were that simple.

Israel and the Jews

See, we have a problem with this deceptively simple logic. Israel is a country which claims most of its citizens-to-be to reside outside its borders. Israel claims that a.) It is a "Jewish country," b.) That all Jews are its potential citizens, c.) That it is OK for her to meddle in the affairs of other countries on behalf of what it thinks are Jewish interests, and, finally, d.) That any opprobrium gained by its actions, resulting in hatred or actual violence directed at those it claims to represent, is derived from racial and irrational causes. This, alas, does not make sense.

This is without even mentioning the hidden point e.), rarely mentioned, which says that Israel thinks it is perfectly acceptable to use Jews living in other countries as its agents.

I'm not just talking about [Israeli-American convicted of spying on the United States for Israel, Jonathan] Pollard here—this goes way, way deeper. For instance, the first semi-public f--k-up of [Israeli] intelligence services came in 1954, when military intelligence activated a terror cell in Egypt, composed of local Jews, which attempted to attack British and American targets for reasons beyond human ken.

When the US does something awful—the invasion of Iraq comes to mind—its standing [in] the world understandably plummets and we hear people speak of anti-Americanism. When Israel does something terrible, anti-Israeli sentiments understandably rise.

However, this is much more complicated. Israel keeps claiming it represents all Jews, even though most of them rejected the Zionist idea and refused to immigrate to Israel. Yet, when people hostile to Israel take it at its word, and act towards Jewish communities as if they were Israeli communities, Israel wails it is anti-Semitism.

It is, of course. The idea that all members of a group are responsible for the actions of other members is racist. But just how did the idea that "Jews" equals "Israelis" come about? Doesn't the Israeli government have something to do with that? Isn't it saying time and time again that Israel is a "Jewish" country?

Goldberg's analogy simply does not work. Saying that all blacks are responsible for the actions of a single criminal, or that this single criminal is an indication that all blacks are criminals, is manifestly racist, but it is nowhere near the mark. Let's try another analogy. Let's say a band of rabid black-supremacists invaded a piece of land, claiming it to be their ancestral homeland, supported by Europeans who wanted those people out of their own country; Let's say the invaders ruthlessly drove back the less organized, under-armed, surprised locals; Let's say they have kept the indigent population as second-class citizens, and later invaded another country and exported those methods to it—all the while claiming to represent black people everywhere, such a farcical claim being taken seriously by many countries. Would anyone be surprised if anti-Black sentiment would rise?

Muslim Anti-semitism

Let's test the hypothesis. If we look at anti-Semitism in the Muslim world, it certainly existed. Jews were considered inferior by law to Muslims in almost all Muslim countries. The myth about the "golden age of Andalus" [in present day Spain from 711–1492], when Jews, Muslims and Christians lived in harmony is, alas, a myth. There are certainly anti-Semitic elements in the various Islamic traditions.

But one would have to be a fool to claim Muslim anti-Semitism held a candle to Christian anti-Semitism. That's where the knives were really out. Jews often describe Christianity as Judaism's wayward daughter; In fact, given that Christianity rose just as rabbinical Judaism was finally affirming itself, they are two squabbling sisters. The tension between them is explosive, because they fought over the meaning of the same symbols and texts. Which is "verus Israel," true Israel? The followers of the Talmud and Rashim, or those whose circumcision was "that of the heart"? Which is it, Passover or Easter? Pentacost or Shavuot? Are we redeemed by the blood of the Lamb, or is the [Passover] blood on doorframe just a fading memory of the delivery from Egypt? It is no coincidence that the blood libel traditionally happens near Easter. Or is it Passover? Which redeeming blood?[1]

The Church preserved well the memory of the early days, when Jews used their power as an established religion to humiliate and persecute the followers of the new, illicit religion. Then came Constantine [a Roman emperor who became Christian], and the wheel turned. The Church turned the other cheek to its own teachings, and the Jews became the

1. These are all comparisons of similar Jewish and Christian traditions.

persecuted—and took the vengeance of the oppressed. In secret books, preserved generation after generation, they poured scorn on Jesus, calling him a magician, calling his mother a whore of the Romans. Time after time, rabbis forbade Jews from spitting on crosses; Time after time, they break the ruling, and sometimes pay a hideous price. The emperor Theodosius has to enact a law, which forbids Jews from portraying the hanging of Haman [an Old Testament persecutor of Jews who was executed] as the crucifixion of Jesus; At least one pogrom [systematic persecution] in the 12th century begins after Jews in France crucify a murderer during Purim celebrations, in lieu of Haman.[2] Then we have the horrifying events of the crusades, with Jews murdering their children to prevent their baptism; And they lead horrified Christians to wonder: If this is what they will do to their own children, if they hate us so much, what will [they] do to our children?

Modern Muslim Anti-Semitism

No, Muslim anti-Semitism doesn't hold a candle to this terrible history. It comes into its own in the 1920s, and it's not an accident. These are the times when the Protocols [of the Elders of Zion, an anti-Semitic forgery]—the last, poisonous gift [of] Czarist Russia, with its most anti-Semitic of churches—are considered to be earth shattering documents, when even the *Times* of London referred to them as holding a possible truth. And look—despite the fact that the Arabs are much more numerous, despite the fact they are more powerful, the Jews are much more influential with the allies, and they carve their own piece of the Arab world for themselves.

That's where Muslim anti-Semitism starts to come into its own: From a conspiracy theory and as a reaction to Zionism [the belief that a state of Israel should be founded]. Hostility to Zionism and the British makes it a very short journey to

---

2. Purim celebrates the deliverance of the Jews from a genocidal plot by Haman during the Persian Empire.

support [Adolf] Hitler. The creation of Israel out of the ruins of Palestine empowers this conspiratorial sort of anti-Semitism, ironically an import of a colonial legacy. The humiliating defeat of 1967 [when Israel defeated Egypt, Jordan, and Syria] further fuels this concept, giving renewed life to political Islamism as Arab nationalism is discredited.

And between these Scylla and Charybdis [an ancient Greek dilemma], between Israel's claim to represent all Jews and the Arab world's embrace of now-discredited Western anti-Semitism, the Jewish communities of the Muslim world are crashed. The ancient Jewish settlements of Egypt and Iraq, which pre-date the Second Temple [ca. 500 B.C., are broken and their members are forced to run for their lives. 2,500 years of existence end in tragedy.

And if, after this, you are still capable of piously saying "anti-Semitism has nothing to do with Israel," you are either not paying attention, or you're not arguing in good faith.

"*To an extent, the exact same metaphors and ideas are used to incite hatred against Muslims as were and are used to incite hatred against Jews.*"

There Are Parallels Between Islamophobia and Anti-Semitism

Sabine Schiffer and Constantin Wagner

Sabine Schiffer is head of the Media Responsibility Institute (IMV) in Erlangen, Germany; Constantin Wagner is a researcher at the Georg Eckert Institute and also works at the IMV. In the following viewpoint, the authors argue that, while anti-Semitism and Islamophobia are not the same, they are comparable in some ways. For instance, the authors say, both Jews and Muslims are singled out for belonging to a religious collective, and both are also vilified as foreigners. And while the position of Muslims in Germany is not comparable to that of the Jews under the Nazis, the authors say, the experience of Nazi Germany also reveals that the Holocaust was enabled by decades of anti-Semitic rhetoric. They conclude that prejudice, including Islamophobia, needs to be confronted and disarmed whenever it appears.

As you read, consider the following questions:

1. Why do some people object to the use of the term *Isla-mophobia*, and how do the authors reply to this objection?

2. What evidence of anti-Semitic attacks and incidents in Germany do Schiffer and Wagner provide?

3. The authors say that Muslims and Jews are viewed as the counterparts to an ideal, but in different ways. What are these ways?

Time and again, the comparison of anti-Semitism and Islamophobia/anti-Muslim racism generates public angst. The high point of this disquiet in Germany surrounded the conference '*Feindbild* Muslim–*Feindbild* Jude' (The Muslim as Enemy, the Jew as Enemy) organised by the Berlin-based Zentrum für Antisemitismusforschung (Centre for the Study of Anti-Semitism) in December 2008.

This reaction to such a comparison is understandable and justified to the extent that there can be real doubts as to whether the horrors of genocidal anti-Semitism—the Nazi Holocaust—should be relativised (that is, on the moral level) and there could be grounds for suspecting that to mention both phenomena in the same breath comes from faulty analysis; for example, if someone claimed that Muslims today were in the same position as Jews had been under Nazi rule. However, it is inappropriate to play Jews and Muslims off against each other as objects of racist discourses; to deny the existence of this new phenomenon of Islamophobia, which does indeed exist, or to dismiss as trivial all expressions of racism that fall short of total barbarism.

To compare is not to equate, as Micha Brumlik (a famous pedagogue who analyses issues of Jewish identity, the Holocaust and anti-Semitism) and others have repeatedly emphasised. Quite the contrary. When comparing, one naturally also examines the differences between two things. To equate anti-Semitism and Islamophobia would not only be a moral problem, but an analytical one as well. But at the same time, reality forces those of us who deal with racism and seek to combat it to consider the phenomenon of Islamophobia. And, to the extent that there are parallels, why should we not try to learn from the findings of research on anti-Semitism?

A few parallels and differences will be examined below. In so doing, it seems useful to distinguish between the analytical/conceptual level on the one hand and the empirical level on the other.

Islamophobia as Cultural Racism

There can be no doubt that, empirically, a phenomenon exists that we describe as 'Islamophobia' and others describe as 'anti-Muslim racism' or 'hostility to Islam'. One criticism of the term 'Islamophobia' has been that it defames opponents of Islamist movements. But even if it is true that the term can be instrumentalised, that is not sufficient cause to stop using it. After all, 'racism', too, has varying definitions, and is occasionally used in highly problematic ways. This does not mean that there is no point in continuing to use the term, and certainly would not justify denying its very existence.

Looking at critical portrayals of Muslims from an anti-racist perspective, there can be no doubt that Islam is openly being attacked as Islam, and Muslims are openly being attacked as Muslims. The same applies to physical violence. Islamophobes often try to legitimise their racism by arguing that they have nothing against 'foreigners' in general, and even add to their credentials by explaining they are 'pro-Israeli'; the problem, they explain, is Muslims. Such Islamophobia has recently begun to be studied in Germany and reported in a number of published pieces on racism and anti-racism.

Given the enormous popularity of blogs such as *Politically Incorrect*, which publishes nothing but racist incitement specifically against Muslims, it is undeniable that there is a racism that is directed primarily at (supposed) Muslims. The known racist blogs are merely the tip of the iceberg, and can build on very widespread, historically based anti-Muslim resentments.

Although many images and points are familiar elements of 'anti-immigration' discourse and thus recognisable as elements of racism, the empirical phenomenon of 'Islamophobia' is not entirely coextensive with the definition of 'racism' (to the extent that there is a universally valid definition of the term). This is because centuries-old anti-Muslim views inform, shape and extend the current discourse. This gives anti-Muslim racism a specificity that distinguishes it from other racisms.

Furthermore, Islamophobia can be considered a new form of racism, a 'cultural racism'. The target of Islamophobia is not an imagined 'race', but a group perceived as a religious community. It is easier to incite hatred using supposed cultural as opposed to 'racial' characteristics and this also affects the intensity and nature of the 'necessary resistance'.

Anti-Semitism as Coherent Racism

Although anti-Semitic attitudes are much more heavily stigmatised in post-Nazi Germany than are other forms of racism, it is by no means true that there is no longer any anti-Semitism. On the one hand, there are phenomena known to researchers as 'secondary anti-Semitism' and 'structural anti-Semitism'. 'Secondary anti-Semitism' refers to the cultivation of resentments against Jews not just by reference to the traditional prejudices that continue to exist, but also by using new motifs. One example of this is the idea that Jews, allegedly, prevent Germany from 'putting its past behind it'. This is an 'updated' form of traditional accusations, such as greed and lust for power. Jews are once again painted as disrupting German national identity—but this time through *Vergangenheits-bewältigung* (the process of coming to terms with the [Nazi] past).

Attitudes in the United States Toward Arabs and Muslims

	Attitude Toward Arabs		Attitude Toward Muslims	
	Favorable	Unfavorable	Favorable	Unfavorable
All Respondents				
2003	46%	35%	47%	32%
2010	43%	40%	35%	55%
2012	41%	39%	40%	41%
Democratic				
2003	50%	29%	55%	33%
2010	57%	30%	54%	34%
2012	48%	29%	49%	29%
Republican				
2003	42%	42%	41%	40%
2010	28%	68%	12%	85%
2012	27%	53%	26%	57%

TAKEN FROM: Arab American Institute, "The American Divide: How We View Arabs and Muslims," August 23, 2012.

'Structural anti-Semitism' refers to ideas that are not explicitly directed at Jews, but are similar to anti-Semitic ideas in their concepts and argument. One example of this is the differentiation between and personification of 'money-grubbing' financial capital and 'working' productive capital (this refers to [Adolf] Hitler's terms 'raffendes/schaffendes Kapital'). This personalising and abbreviation of Marxist social criticism is structurally anti-Semitic and can also promote hostility towards Jews.

On the other hand, there are still explicitly anti-Semitic statements being made and attacks taking place. In 2008,

1,089 anti-Semitic crimes were recorded in Germany. Between 2000 and 2008, approximately 470 desecrations of Jewish cemeteries were recorded. Approximately 10 per cent of all Germans agree with anti-Semitic statements, such as that Jews have too much influence, Jews are more likely to use underhanded methods than others, or that Jews are peculiar and do not quite fit in with 'us'.

While such views may not be held across the board, there is a definite tendency for abuse of Jews to be expressed less openly and explicitly than other prejudices. In Germany, there is a stigma attached to propounding clear anti-Semitic views and to attacks on Jews (as Jews)—although this taboo is occasionally broken. Post-Shoah [Holocaust], anti-Semitism in Germany is mostly indirect, overwhelmingly in the form of secondary and structural anti-Semitism. Muslims, on the other hand, are abused more openly than any other marked group.

To claim that fear of Muslims—unlike fear of Jews—is legitimised by referring to Islamic fundamentalism, does not pass muster. This use of alleged fact is, in itself, racist, because it rests on a fundamental, racist generalisation—the acts of very few individuals are explained in terms of their religious background and then attributed collectively to all Muslims. This group is evaluated based on the accumulation of (negative) facts. This pattern is familiar from other racist discourses, including, in particular, anti-Semitism. Anti-Semitic discourse is the example par excellence of how an apparently coherent racist system—which appears to be regularly confirmed—can arise over centuries.

Parallels, Similarities, and Divergences

Collective constructions, dehumanisation, misinterpretation of religious imperatives (proof by 'sources'), and conspiracy theories are the patterns that we find in both anti-Semitic and Islamophobic discourses. The frighteningly clear parallels are unmistakable when one analyses styles of argument and even images. To an extent, the exact same metaphors and ideas are used to incite hatred against Muslims as were and are used to incite hatred against Jews. This can be seen in the many parallel terms, such as 'Islamisation' and 'Judaisation'.

Particularly in times of crisis, identity can be constructed by designating subjects and groups that allegedly constitute an internal and/or external threat as 'foreign'. While it was already a classic anti-Semitic motif in the nineteenth century that 'the Jews' identified with 'their race' and not with the country of which they were citizens, we see a similar motif in the discussions of 'Muslim parallel societies'. This goes so far as to reactivate the clearly anti-Semitic metaphor of 'a state within a state', this time in relation to Muslims. In this way, the fact that one belongs to a religious community becomes a total identification, as if 'being Muslim' were the sole and decisive factor explaining all of a Muslim person's actions and attitudes.

Despite the commonalities in the arguments and argumentational styles, there is a difference on the conceptual and analytical level between the internal logic of 'anti-Semitism' and of 'Islamophobia'.

Both Jews and Muslims have historically been perceived as a danger for 'the Christian West', though in differing ways. The 'Turks at the gates of Vienna' (part of collective memory) has long been a popular motif both in relation to the immigration of Muslims and with regard to 'Islamisation'. The Moors in Spain were always 'foreign' in the sense of 'outsiders'. Opposing them and driving them out was not only permissible, it was required. Thus, they fit the classic notion of the foreigner in the racist worldview—the external, visible enemy. Jews, on the other hand, were primarily viewed as an 'internal' enemy. Modern anti-Semitism faced an enemy which was 'invisible'—because of assimilation. This was combined with the idea of destroyers from within who needed to be exterminated rather than driven out. Thus, the Crusades were directed against an actual and/or perceived external enemy, while anti-Judaism and anti-Semitism were directed inward. In this regard, anti-Semitism is located on a different historical continuum from Islamophobia.

Furthermore, it should be noted that Muslims tend to be viewed as inferior, while anti-Semites generally view Jews as superior. Thus, Jews were always considered the representatives of modernism, whether in the form of liberalism, capitalism, or communism, while Muslims are perceived as 'backwardness' incarnate. Here it can be seen that both Muslims and Jews are seen as the counterpart to an ideal, though in different ways. Additionally, there are differences with regard to explanatory content. Anti-Semitic discourse seeks to explain not only a part of reality (as do other racist discourses) but the entire world. Thus, 'the Jew' can be seen to be pulling the strings of virtually any evil: capitalism and communism, Washington and Moscow, godlessness and the most devout faith. Anti-Semitism is a total, universal theory.

It is important to understand these differences in order to be able to unpick and combat the respective analyses. However, the differences in resentment—against inferiors, on the one hand, from those perceived as omnipotent, on the other, between the external and internal enemy—relate to a conceptual level. Things are not always this clear in (racist) reality.

Empirical Shifts

Although this analytical distinction still tends to be valid, there have recently been empirical shifts that make it more and more necessary to use findings from the study of anti-Semitism to analyse Islamophobia.

In addition to being represented as the external enemy, Muslims appear more and more as the 'internal' enemy in racist discourse, a figure most clearly personified, even today, by 'the Jew'. This can be seen in the treatment of Islamism as a matter of internal security. A growing number of Muslims are

German citizens, and therefore no longer 'foreigners' or 'external enemies'. Additionally, more and more Muslims are targeted by accusations that they are 'in camouflage', particularly those who seek to participate actively in civil society or professional life. They are presumed to be loyal to 'their own group', based on their religion. This breaks through the traditional classification, with Muslims now being promoted to an 'internal enemy' in the paranoid imagination.

The idea of the superior privileging of the 'Other' is applied more and more frequently to Muslims. The debates about 'special rights', whether with regard to the right to wear a headscarf at work or participation at school, show no sign of stopping. Both in popular debates and in various publications, the idea is being expressed that Germany is being 'Islamised', with substantial financial support from the 'Near East', through the purchasing of land, building of mosques, and influence in the media.

Islamophobic conspiracy theories are quite popular in the relevant blogs. These conspiracy theories do indeed seek to explain various political developments, and not just individual phenomena. While a closed anti-Semitic worldview begins from an attempt to explain the world, in the case of Islamophobia, there is the tendency to explain more and more facts from social life by reference to the religious background of Muslims. Thus, any number of problems, from youth violence to homophobia, appear to be explicable by reference to 'Islam'.

Based on these shifts and adoptions, we must acknowledge that other marked groups may also fall into the role historically assigned primarily to Jews—an element of negation that destroys healthy collectives. This requires, first of all, a group that is 'marked' as such. Today, we see that actual and apparent Muslims are perceived 'as Muslims' with increasing intensity. Concepts like ethnic pluralism (towards the Right end of the spectrum) and multiculturalism (which tends to be used on the Left) can even help along this racist process of marking out a religious group as 'the Other'.

This practice of marking, in itself, must be understood as a racist thought pattern that leads to further steps of attributing negative characteristics, defamation and discrimination. The act of physical racial violence carried out by an individual is the end product of a whole process of racialisation which begins with the stereotypes that society as a whole generates and perpetuates through laws, the media, the education system, and so on, in popular discourse.

The Holocaust as a Warning

Among other things, anti-Semitism and Islamophobia differ in post-Nazi Germany with regard to the degree of openness with which they are expressed. And, in terms of 'traditional' interpretations of racism, they have separate—one might say complementary—functions. In this regard, it is important to examine the differences in how anti-Semitism and Islamophobia operate analytically; this also helps in discovering the ways in which they shift and how they get adopted. Both phenomena exist empirically, and have a function as racist—false— explanations of the world.

It is obviously absurd to claim that Muslims today are in the same situation as Jews were 'back then'. In comparing anti-Semitism and Islamophobia, we should not relativise the Nazi Holocaust—instead, the goal should be to recognise racist mechanisms before even the threat of a comparable situation arises. The thesis that the Nazi Holocaust, while historically singular, is capable of repetition is not a new one in the study of anti-Semitism and the Shoah. The fact that we must assume that a total catastrophe is capable of repetition must be treated separately from the fact that the Shoah is a historically singular phenomenon, and that victims and perpetrators can be named specifically.

However, memory alone will not suffice, particularly because we know today that the destruction of the Jews in the Third Reich would not have been possible without a decades-long and centuries-old preparatory anti-Semitic discourse. Based on the historical imperative to deconstruct racist discourse before it is too late, a racist discourse that threatens to become highly dominant in society must be exposed as such. To this end, we must also expose and analyse the occasionally frightening parallels to anti-Semitic discourse. While there is still evidence of anti-Semitic explanatory styles and resentments, anti-Islamic voices are becoming more and more influential in public discourse.

The achievement in the study of anti-Semitism of examining Jewry and anti-Semitism separately must also be transferred to other racisms, such as Islamophobia. We do not need more information about Islam, but more information about the making of racist stereotypes in general. In order to do this, it is necessary to understand that the ideas and images of a 'foreign group' say more about the group that produces them than about the group marked as the 'out group'.

> "There is no other prejudice or form of racism which you can compare to anti-Semitism."

Anti-Semitism Isn't Islamophobia

Phyllis Chesler

Phyllis Chesler is the cofounder of the Association of Women in Psychology and the author of The New Anti-Semitism. *In the following viewpoint, she argues that anti-Semitism cannot be compared to Islamophobia. This is because, Chesler says, Jews have been persecuted in Europe for thousands of years for no reason; Muslims, on the other hand, have been in Europe in large numbers only for decades and deliberately threaten Western values. She further argues that antipathy to Muslims is justified, while antipathy to Jews is irrational hatred, and concludes that the two should never be compared.*

As you read, consider the following questions:

1. What does Chesler feel Muslims would have to do to show that they were in good faith in condemning anti-Semitism?

2. Why does Clemens Heni, as cited by the author, argue that there is justification for Islamophobia?

3. What does Chesler say happened to Jews in Muslim Spain?

Did you know that Jews and Muslims have a shared history in Europe? That Muslims have "deep roots" on the European continent and that Muslims are as imperiled by "Islamophobia" as Jews are by anti-Semitism?

Nothing could be further from the truth, and yet the first Gathering of European Muslim and Jewish Leaders issued a statement on May 9th and just held a meeting in Brussels on May 30, 2011.

Oddly enough, the meeting was organized by two American Jewish groups, Rabbi Marc Schneier's Foundation For Ethnic Understanding and philanthropist Ronald Lauder's World Jewish Congress, as well as by the European Jewish Congress.

No Muslim organization seems to have shared in organizing the meeting, although two organizations and more than a dozen Muslim leaders attended and signed the joint declaration.

Can you believe this? Is this some kind of exercise in dhimmitude and self-delusion? Why are the Jews doing the heavy lifting for the far wealthier Muslim world? More important: Why support such dangerously misguided concepts?

At this moment in world history, why are Jews confusing "Islamophobia" with anti-Semitism? One understands that Muslims might want to assume whatever is left of Jewish victimhood and make it their own—but why are Jews enabling them to do so?

If the Muslims are coming in great good faith, they would state some obvious truths, beginning with the Koranic roots of Jew- and infidel-hatred and the contemporary Islamist/genocidal intentions towards the Jewish State.

Indeed, a new kind of statement from Muslims would include their understanding of—and desire to break from—the historical Muslim persecution of Jews and infidels in Muslim-majority countries.

This is not that kind of statement or declaration.

Anti-Semitism cannot, must not, be equated with Islamophobia. European Muslims have nothing to fear from European Jews. European Jews have everything to fear from European Muslims.

As Clemens Heni, a scholar of German anti-Semitism, has pointed out: "There is no other prejudice or form of racism which you can compare to anti-Semitism. If you look at Islam today, there is a (reason for) Islamophobia because Jihadists say, 'We want to kill the unbelievers.' Jews never said that." Those who equate legitimate fears of Islamist extremism with anti-Semitism, he argues, clearly "didn't learn the lesson [of] the Holocaust. They are even downplaying the Holocaust itself."

According to the declaration, "Jews and Muslims live side-by-side in every European country and our two communities are important components of Europe's religious, cultural and social tapestry." The document fails to mention that those Jews who live "side-by-side" with Muslims are in danger of being harassed, beaten, or even tortured to death, as was Ilan Halimi of France.

The declaration commits an outrage against history by equating the Jewish experience in Europe with the Muslim experience in Europe, even though Jews have been living as a persecuted minority on the continent for more than a thousand years while most Muslims only arrived in large numbers after World War II. The declaration lumps together the Shoah (Holocaust), the slaughter of six million Jews, with the mass killings of some thousands of Muslims in Bosnia during the 1990s.

It ignores the history of Muslim Spain in the Middle Ages, when both Christian and Muslim rulers persecuted Jews and Muslim mobs slaughtered them in pogroms. Needless to say, no Jewish outrages against Christian or Muslim communities have ever taken place on European soil.

With mock solemnity, the document proclaims, "We must never allow anti-Semitism . . . to become respectable in today's Europe"—as if anti-Semitism, in its modern guise of anti-Zionism, weren't already perfectly respectable in every corner of Europe.

Rabbis all over Europe have been telling their people to flee before it is too late. Many Jews have done so.

Why is a group of Jews trying to help Muslims, however fine, by appealing to European governments not to "pander to right wing forces" which are, belatedly, beginning to gather in response to a Muslim population which is hostile to Western and European values, does not wish to assimilate, and is both separatist and violent?

Had Muslims come in total peace these "right wing forces" may have, indeed, been a reflection of European racism towards Arabs and dark-skinned "Easterners." But the alleged "Islamophobia" is not based on bigoted considerations of color, faith, or ethnicity; it is, rather, based on the increasing danger that Muslims pose to the stability and character of Europe.

Will these Muslim signatories agree to a declaration that critiques Iran, Saudi Arabia, the Muslim Brotherhood in Egypt and in Gaza, and Palestinians in general, for their hatred of Israel, the Jewish state? If not, what is to be gained by standing in solidarity with such Muslims?

According to Clemens Heni, the views of this declaration:

Definitely [do] not represent the Jewish community in Germany—neither the Central Council of Jews in Germany nor any important Jewish Community Center supports this (nonsense). Muslims did not at all live as long in Europe as

Jews did. Muslims and Germans declared Jihad in November 1914, during the First World War. THIS is what the German-Muslim alliance in the 20th century is all about.

In Heni's view, the Muslim "history" in Europe is about Muslim anti-Semitic alliances with German and Nazi anti-Semites.

Who are the Jewish "leaders" who organized and attended this meeting? Who appointed them? Are they this desperate for headlines or so eager to be seen as "players"? Are they so genuinely frightened for their endangered European communities that they are willing to say and do anything, or are they simply dangerously misguided?

It is the midnight hour. What kinds of private deals and illusions are these leaders conjuring up for themselves?

Periodical and Internet Sources Bibliography

The following articles have been selected to supplement the diverse views presented in this chapter.

Andrew Brown   "Islamphobia and Antisemitism," *The Guardian* (Manchester, UK), June 27, 2011.

Phyllis Chesler and Nathan Bloom   "Why Can Academics Study 'Islamophobia' but Not Anti-Semitism?," *FrontPage Magazine*, June 27, 2011. http://frontpagemag.com/2011/ phyllis-chesler-and-nathan-bloom/why-can -academics-study-islamophobia-but-not-anti -semitism.

Jason Hill   "The Myth of Islamophobia," *The Shepherd* (blog), Open Salon, July 11, 2012. http:// open.salon.com/blog/jason_d_hill/2012/07 /11/the_myth_of_islamophobia.

Idrees   "Muslim Anti-Semitism: Myth and Reality," Pulse, July 4, 2012. http://pulsemedia.org/2012 /07/04/36427.

Richard Landes   "Muslim Anti-Semitism, Israel, and the Dynamics of Self-Destructive Scapegoating," CiF Watch, March 17, 2012. http://cifwatch.com/ 2012/03/17/muslim-anti-semitism-israel-and -the-dynamics-of-self-destructive-scapegoating.

Sheila Musaji   "Islamophobia & Anti-Semitism, Everything Old Is New Again," Loonwatch.com, June 25, 2012. www.loonwatch.com/2012/06/ islamophobia-anti-semitism-everything-old-is -new-again.

David Turner   "Foundations of Antisemitism: Augustine and Christian Triumphalism," *Jerusalem Post*, blogs, August 2, 2012. http://blogs.jpost.com/content/ foundations-antisemitism-augustine-and -christian-triumphalism.

Is Opposition to Israeli Policy Linked to Anti-Semitism?

Chapter Preface

Israel has an extremely tense relationship with its regional neighbor, Iran. In recent years, Iran has been accused of seeking to develop a nuclear weapon. This has served only to further inflame the relationship with Israel.

Part of the reason for the intensity of Israeli/Iranian conflict has been the outspoken anti-Semitism of Iran's Islamic leadership. For example, in a July 12, 2012, article for Jewish social and political magazine *Commentary*, Jonathan Tobin notes that Iran's vice president delivered a speech at a United Nations conference in which he blamed Jews for the international drug trade. Tobin also says that the Iranian government sponsored a contest in which Iranians were urged to create cartoons that both denied the Holocaust and mocked its victims. Tobin concludes:

> Foreign policy realists who think a nuclear Iran can be contained or that it can be trusted not to use nukes simply ignore the incitement and hatred against Jews that is commonplace in Iranian culture. Similarly, those who believe diplomacy can sweet talk the ayatollahs [Islamic leaders] into giving up their nuclear ambitions are not taking into account the way their enmity for Jews has come to define Iran's view of the world.

Similarly, Colbert I. King, writing in an August 3, 2012, essay in the *Washington Post*, explicitly compares the Iranian regime to the Nazis and suggests that Iran wants to commit "genocide" against Jews and Israel. Adam Garfinkle in a June 29, 2012, article at the *American Interest* also emphasizes the seriousness of Iranian anti-Semitism and cites it as a reason that diplomacy will not work. Instead, he suggests, the United States will eventually have to take "kinetic" action—by which he means that it will have to use armed force against Iran.

Other writers, however, have challenged the idea that Iranian anti-Semitism necessitates, or points to the need for, a military intervention in the region. Philip Giraldi, in a December 15, 2011, post at Antiwar.com, states, "No matter how one feels about Iran's government and its ambitions, everyone should be taking notice of what is happening to fuel the drive to war." He argues that the charge of anti-Semitism has been used to smear anyone who criticizes Israel, or who does not agree that a war with Iran is necessary or wise. He believes that these charges of anti-Semitism, and the push for war, are dangerous and immoral and will ultimately damage the Middle East, Israel, and the United States.

Naomi Lipsky, writing in a December 7, 2012, article at *The Jewish Voice and Herald*, argues that a war against Iran might actually cause serious harm to the Jewish community living in Iran. Lipsky writes:

> The position of Jews in Iran today remains a unique one. Interviews of Iranian Jews by the media show people living normal, comfortable lives. The Iranian constitution of 1906 mandated that minorities were entitled to representation in Parliament; since then, there has always been one Jewish member of the Parliament. The government today is rabidly anti-Israel and anti-Zionist, but professes no sanctions against Jews who are not Zionists. When Mahmoud Ahmadinejad, the Iranian president from 2005 to 2013, made one of his many speeches denying the Holocaust, the Jewish member of Parliament at the time, Maurice (Morris) Mohtamid, wrote a letter of protest and did not suffer any repercussions.

Lipsky says that some Iranian Jews worry that a war with Israel will make them a target for violence and prejudice. She quotes one Iranian Jew as saying, "So far, things are good, but God knows what will happen tomorrow."

The conflict between Israel and Iran is only one of many ways in which discussions of Israel are linked to discussions of anti-Semitism. In the viewpoints in this chapter, writers take opposing stances as to when, how, and whether, opposition to Israel is tied to anti-Semitism.

> "Whoever—Jew or non-Jew—advances
> a campaign against the well-being or
> the existence of the Jewish state is, quite
> simply, an anti-Semite."

Anti-Zionism Is Anti-Semitism

David Solway

David Solway is a Canadian poet and writer. In the following viewpoint, he argues that anti-Zionism, or opposition to the existence or expansion of the state of Israel, is merely a cover for anti-Semitism. He argues that Jews who oppose Zionism do so because they want to assimilate into their surrounding culture and forget their heritage; he contends that they ultimately erase their own identity and concludes that criticism of Israel is acceptable but says it should be carefully framed so as not to oppose Zionism. Anyone who does oppose Zionism, he maintains, whether Christian, Muslim, or Jew, is anti-Semitic.

As you read, consider the following questions:

1. What did Martin Luther King Jr. say about anti-Zionism, according to Solway?

2. In what fantasy are anti-Zionist Jews living, in the author's opinion?

3. Of what does Solway say that anti-Zionists despoil the Jewish people?

It is easy to see that many critics of Israel are unquestionably anti-Semitic in outlook and feeling and are merely using a political argument to camouflage a religious, racist, or ethnophobic sentiment. Under cover of "legitimate criticism of Israel" and the condemnation of Zionism [Jewish nationalism] as an invasive colonial movement, anti-Semitism has now become safe. Plainly, the distinction these new anti-Semites like to draw between anti-Semitism as such and anti-Zionism is intended only to cloak the fundamental issue and to provide camouflage for vulgar ideas and beliefs.

Unqualified Anti-Semitism

This is a very shrewd tactic and is most disconcerting not only in its vindictiveness but in its frequency. Jewish philosopher and theologian Emil Fackenheim has outlined three stages of anti-Semitism: "You cannot live among us as Jews," leading to forced conversions; "You cannot live among us," leading to mass deportations; and "You cannot live," leading to genocide. Amnon Rubinstein, patron of the Israeli Shinui party and author of *From Herzl to Rabin: The Changing Image of Zionism*, has added a fourth stage: "You cannot live in a state of your own," which leads to boycott, divestment, sanctions, biased reporting, *pro forma* support of the Palestinians, and calls for the delegitimation, territorial reduction, and in some cases even the disappearance of Israel as we know it.

If this is not unqualified anti-Semitism, then nothing is. As Martin Luther King Jr. observed at a Harvard book fair during which Zionism came under assault: "It is the denial to the Jewish people of a fundamental right that we justly claim for the people of Africa and freely accord all other nations of the Globe. It is discrimination against Jews, my friend, because they are Jews. In short, it is anti-Semitism. . . . Let my words echo in the depths of your soul: When people criticize Zionism, they mean Jews—make no mistake about it." King understood, as so many have not, that there is really no daylight between anti-Zionism and anti-Semitism. To deprive Jews of their national haven or to submerge them in a so-called "binational state" with an Arab majority is to render them vulnerable to prejudicial fury, scapegoating, pogroms, and, ultimately, even to Holocaust.

King's homespun analysis has been confirmed in a report released in the August 2006 issue of the *Journal of Conflict Resolution* by the Yale School of Management in collaboration with its Institute for Social and Policy Studies. The report concludes that the statistical link between anti-Zionism and anti-Semitism can no longer be denied—a correlation that should have been obvious years ago despite the disclaimers regularly circulated by covert Jew-haters and Jewish revisionists.

In *Why The Jews?* Dennis Prager and Joseph Telushkin similarly point out that:

> the contention that anti-Zionists are not enemies of Jews, despite the advocacy of policies that would lead to the mass murder of Jews, is, to put it as generously as possible, disingenuous.... Given, then, that if anti-Zionism realized its goal, another Jewish holocaust would take place, attempts to draw distinctions between anti-Zionism and antisemitism are simply meant to fool the naïve.

A Change in Rhetoric

All that has happened, according to these authors, is "only a change in rhetoric." Anti-Zionism, they claim, "is unique in only one way: it is the first form of Jew-hatred to deny that it hates the Jews."

When we turn to the Jewish community itself, we find an analogous dynamic at work among many of its more fractious and insensible members. The issue is only exacerbated by the

Seventy years of progress

© Loren Fishman/lfin266/cartoonstock.com.

large number of generally left-wing Jews who have spoken out against Israel, levelling an endless barrage of cavils, reproofs, and aspersions against social and political conditions in the Jewish state or its negotiation tactics vis à vis the Palestinians. The verbal Kassams [rockets launched against Israel] and textual Katyushas [artillery] they continually launch are as damaging to Israel's international standing as [Palestinian militant group] Hamas rockets and [Lebanon-based Islamic militant group] Hezbollah missiles are to its physical security. Some go so far as to deplore its very existence, regarding the country as a burden on their assimilationist lifestyle, as an unwelcome reminder of their indelible and resented Jewishness, or as a particularist violation of their utopian notions of universal justice.

Many Jews tend to see Israel as a threat to their convenience, a nuisance at best, a peril at worst. They have failed to comprehend the justice of [philosopher and literary critic] George Steiner's lambent remark in *Language and Silence*: "If Israel were to be destroyed, no Jew would escape unscathed. The shock of failure, the need and harrying of those seeking refuge, would reach out to implicate even the most indifferent, the most anti-Zionist." According to [author] Saul Bellow in *To Jerusalem and Back*, the great Israeli historian Jacob Leib Talmon was of the same mind. In a conversation with the author, Talmon feared that the destruction of Israel would bring with it the end of "corporate Jewish existence all over the world, and a catastrophe that might overtake U.S. Jewry."

These Jews who are vexed by the existence of their fallback country are living in a fantasy of personal immunity to the bubonics [plagues] of Jew-hatred, something that has never ceased to infect the world. In reviling the one nation on earth that serves as a last asylum should they ever find themselves *in extremis*, they have not only risked their—or their children's—possible future survival. They have also effectively expunged their own historical identity, aligning themselves with the foul theories and convictions of their persecutors. *Victim and victimizer are in agreement.* This is nothing less than a form of self-loathing, a rejection of essence, that paradoxically corresponds to the contempt and hatred of the non-Jewish anti-Semite. It is, in short, nothing less than *reflexive anti-Semitism*.

Jews Must Support Israel

As Daniel Greenfield asks in an article exposing the campus betrayals of the Berkeley Hillel [Jewish campus ministry] chapter that endorses patently anti-Zionist organizations, "why shouldn't there be a consensus that Jewish identity is incompatible with the rejection of the Jewish state?" Following the same line of thought, Phil Orenstein, a member of the National Conference on Jewish Affairs, writes:

For two millennium [sic], the Jewish people have been re-jected from countries throughout the world. Now at long last we have the Jewish State, a safe haven that can welcome our people home. We need to teach our youth what the blessing of Israel means to the Jewish people.

In fact, it is not only Jewish youth who have strayed from the recognition of who they are and who the world regards them as being, as if they could find sanctuary in ostensibly ex-alted ideals or in collaboration with their diehard adversaries. It is every Jew who has embraced the anti-Zionist canard [lie] and by so doing negated his own integrity and selfhood. In denouncing or repudiating Israel, the state founded to ensure his perseverance and preserve his identity in the world, he has renounced that same identity. He has disavowed and thus erased himself—precisely as the typical anti-Zionist, laboring to obliterate Israel from the map, has sought to render the Jew defenseless and susceptible to repression or, even worse, exter-mination.

Updating the Hannukah story, Steven Plaut accurately de-scribes these anti-Zionist Jews as modern Hellenists "ashamed of their Jewishness," siding with the Seleucid empire against the Hasmoneans who fought for the restoration and survival of the Jewish people. But the upshot is that *anyone* who ob-jects to the existence of the state of Israel, who would like to have it vanish from the international stage, who wishes it had never been established, who considers it a geopolitical blun-der, or who insists on treating it as an embarrassment or a nettle to one's equanimity, is an antisemite, for he would de-spoil the Jewish people of its last line of defense in an always problematic world. In *What Is Judaism?*, Fackenheim laments that "all anti-Zionism, Jewish and Gentile, should have come to a total end with the gas chambers and smoke-stacks of Auschwitz." Regrettably, this was not to be.

Certainly, one can be critical of Israel, but given its belea-guered condition, surrounded by enemies and constantly under attack, such criticism must be tempered by respect and circumspection. Nor should criticism function as a stalking horse behind which an inimical or incendiary project moves forward. It is when legitimate criticism morphs into anti-Zionism that we know a malign agenda is at work.

King was right. "When people criticize Zionism, they mean Jews—make no mistake about it." It amounts to the same thing. Whoever—Jew or non-Jew—advances a campaign against the well-being or the existence of the Jewish state is, quite simply, an anti-Semite. It makes no difference if the hater is a Muslim like Sheikh Yusuf al-Qaradawi, a Christian like Jostein Gaarder, an American Jew like Thomas Friedman, or an Israeli Jew like Neve Gordon, he is an enemy of the so-called "Zionist entity" and therefore an anti-Semite. Make no mistake about it.

| "It is not accurate to say that most anti-
Zionists are anti-Semites."

Anti-Zionism Is
Not Anti-Semitism

Lex Rofes

Lex Rofes is a senior in Judaic Studies at Brown University and the president of the Brown chapter of Hillel (a prominent Jewish campus organization), as well as a member of the Hillel International board. In the following viewpoint, he discusses attending a conference of AIPAC, the American Israel Public Affairs Committee, a pro-Zionist lobbying organization. Rofes says that many people at the conference equated anti-Semitism and anti-Zionism. He, though himself a Zionist, argues that this is dangerous, as many American Jews oppose the state of Israel for numerous reasons. He concludes that such disagreement should not be equated with bigotry.

As you read, consider the following questions:

1. What positive experiences did Rofes say he had at the AIPAC conference?

2. According to the author, what was wrong with the focus on Iran at the AIPAC conference?

3. For what reasons may Jews oppose Zionism, in the opinion of Rofes?

This Saturday night [in October 2012], I embarked on a journey that was perhaps long overdue. I participated in an important Jewish life cycle event that seems to have become as vital as a Bar Mitzvah or a wedding. This weekend, I went to my first AIPAC [American Israel Public Affairs Committee—a powerful Jewish lobbying organization] conference ever, the 2012 AIPAC Summit in Boston.

Learning at AIPAC

Walking into the first plenary [full-assembly] session, I was largely unsure of what was about to occur. Of course, as an engaged member of the Jewish community, I am aware of AIPAC's stances on many important Middle East issues. I often disagree with those stances, but I was not at the Summit to stubbornly insist on the correctness of my own opinions, and instead I genuinely hoped to walk away with some new knowledge and understanding.

In some ways, my hopes were fulfilled. John Baird, Canada's Minister of Foreign Affairs, offered a detailed description of Canada's relationship to Israel, a piece of the puzzle to which Americans are often left unexposed. AIPAC honored Judy Feld Carr, a fascinating woman who rescued thousands of Syrian Jews over the course of a few decades, and the presentation left most in the audience feeling quite moved.

However, there were a number of truly disappointing trends I noticed at the summit. Many of the speakers felt that simply stating, "Iran cannot be allowed to obtain a nuclear weapon," in multiple ways constituted a legitimately nuanced and interesting speech. Admittedly, many speakers were politi-

Which Qualities Do American Jews Say Is Most Important to Their Jewish Identity?

When asked which quality is most important to their Jewish identity, nearly half of American Jews cite a commitment to social equality—nearly twice as many as cite support for Israel or religious observance.

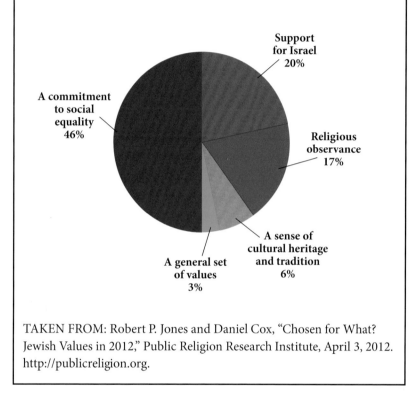

TAKEN FROM: Robert P. Jones and Daniel Cox, "Chosen for What? Jewish Values in 2012," Public Religion Research Institute, April 3, 2012. http://publicreligion.org.

cians currently in the midst of intense campaigns, and they were simply saying what the audience wanted to hear. That said, from politicians such as Congressman David Cicilline and Senator Sheldon Whitehouse, two of my own representatives in Rhode Island, I've come to expect far more. While Iran is certainly an issue of vital importance to Israel and to the world, it should never be true that Iranian politics are discussed more than Israeli politics at a summit on the America-Israel relationship.

Anti-Zionists Are Not Bigots

Another disturbing statement I heard repeated again and again was the idea that anti-Zionism is "the new anti-Semitism." This sentiment is incredibly dangerous for a variety of reasons. First, and most relevant to those of us on college campuses, there are many young Jews who identify as anti-Zionist. In the past week, I've had conversations with two personal friends of mine who connect to their Jewish identity in a very real way but who legitimately believe that Israel does not have the right to exist. If their anti-Zionism is anti-Semitism, should I be thinking of these friends of mine as self-hating Jews? Should I be encouraging them to seek counseling for their irrational ways of thinking?

While I personally believe that Israel should exist as a Jewish state, I would not place myself on the moral high ground and say that those who disagree with me are bigots, nor would most college students. The reality of the situation is that there are many different reasons that people think Israel should not exist. Certainly, there are individuals that don't like Jews and therefore would like for Jews not to have a state. However, many people, especially young Jewish people, have other reasons for not wanting Israel to exist.

Philosophically, they may believe that separation of religion and state is such a vital component of government and therefore any government that incorporates theocratic aspects should be changed. Morally, they may believe that Israel's government has committed acts that place it outside the realm of acceptable behavior, regardless of its Jewish nature. From a utilitarian perspective, they may simply postulate that Israel's existence does not lead to the greatest good for the greatest number, and that a one-state Palestine solution, though harmful to many Israeli lives, may in fact create a world with fewer unnecessary deaths and less paranoia. I disagree with all three of those arguments, and that's part of why I identify as pro-

Israel. But would I feel comfortable calling my friends who make those arguments anti-Semites? Absolutely not.

While we on the left occasionally go overboard with our criticisms of AIPAC, I do believe that the equivocation [*sic*] of Anti-Zionism with Anti-Semitism is profoundly dangerous. While I believe it is true that most anti-Semites are anti-Zionists, it is not accurate to say that most anti-Zionists are anti-Semites. I would hope AIPAC and other organizations take that to heart and find ways that they can nuance their messages in order to avoid slippery generalizations.

> *"Every generation has seen accusations that Jews ... secretly control political structures. ... This is the way [anti-Semitism] always begins."*

Seeds of Anti-Semitism

Michael Gerson

Michael Gerson is a former speechwriter for President George W. Bush and an op-ed columnist for the Washington Post. *In the following viewpoint, he argues that scholars Stephen Walt and John Mearsheimer are wrong to argue that Israel and supporters of Israel have unduly influenced the foreign policy of the United States. On the contrary, he asserts, Israel mostly disagreed with the foreign policy of George W. Bush. He also says that the Bush administration was never influenced by Christian evangelical supporters of Israel, despite the assertions of Walt and Mearsheimer. Gerson concludes that the "Israel Lobby" allegations are dangerous because they mirror anti-Semitic conspiracy theories about Jewish power.*

As you read, consider the following questions:

1. Why does Gerson imply that Walt and Mearsheimer were not really "saying the unsayable"?

2. What was the main Middle East policy initiative of the Bush administration, and why were the Israelis skeptical about it, according to Gerson?

3. Why does the author believe that Americans support Israel?

L ast year [in 2006], Stephen Walt of Harvard and John Mearsheimer of the University of Chicago published a paper accusing the "Israel Lobby" of having "unmatched power" and managing to "manipulate the American political system" into actions that undermine U.S. interests.

George W. Bush and Democracy

Supporters praised these scholars for "prying the lid off a debate that has been bottled up for decades"—perhaps since Charles Lindbergh[1] let down his side of the argument in the 1940s. Another reviewer commends them for "saying the unsayable." In this case, the unsayable was punished with a book advance of three-quarters of a million dollars and turned into 350 pages called *The Israel Lobby and U.S. Foreign Policy.*

Accusations of disproportionate Jewish influence are as old as the pharaohs. The novelty here is the endorsement of respected, mainstream academics—though both characterizations are increasingly disputed. Scholars, not columnists, will make those determinations. But I do have firsthand knowledge concerning two of Walt and Mearsheimer's accusations.

First, they have argued that the "Israeli government and pro-Israel groups" have shaped President [George W.] Bush's "grand scheme for reordering the Middle East."

In fact, Israeli officials have been consistently skeptical about the main policy innovation of the Bush era: the democracy agenda. One senior Bush administration official recently

---

1. Charles Lindbergh flew the first solo flight across the Atlantic Ocean (from New York to Paris) and was considered a national hero. He gained later notoriety for opposing the US entry into World War II and for making statements considered anti-Semitic.

told me, "The Israelis are generally convinced that Arab cultures are particularly resistant to democracy; that democracy is likely to lead to victories by the Muslim Brotherhood."

A friend recalls visiting a prominent Israeli general in 2003 and making the case for democracy promotion. "What is the alternative?" the American asked. "Propping up the next generation of Mubaraks, Assads and the House of Saud for the next 25 years?"[2] The general responded: "Why not?"

President Bush's emphasis on democracy has been driven not by outside pressure but by a strategic insight. He is convinced that the status quo of tyranny, stagnation and extremism in the Middle East is not sustainable—that the rage and ideologies it produces will cause increasing carnage in the world. The eventual solution to this problem, in his view, is the proliferation of hopeful, representative societies in the Middle East.

This argument is debatable. But it is at least as likely as Walt and Mearsheimer's naive belief that "the U.S. has a terrorism problem in good part because it is so closely allied with Israel"—the equivalent of arguing that Britain had a Nazi problem in the 1930s because it was so closely allied with Czechoslovakia.

The Way Anti-Semitism Begins

Second, these scholars contend that the influence within the Bush administration of the Israel lobby has been magnified by its "junior partner," the Christian Zionists. In theological terms, they are talking about premillennial dispensationalists—people who believe that the success of the state of Israel is a welcome sign of the end times.

The views of dispensationalists are broadly disputed by serious, conservative Protestant scholars. I don't share those views. I can't imagine that the president or the secretary of

2. Hosni Mubarek of Egypt, Basharal-Assad of Syria, and the House of Saud in Saudi Arabia, all led (or lead) dictatorial governments supported by the United States.

state shares them—but I would not know for sure because I never once heard such views advocated or mentioned in five years of policy discussions I participated in at the White House.

There is a temptation in some academic circles to search for that mysterious key that will unlock our whole understanding of American foreign policy. George Bush is captive to the Israelis, or maybe [Bush's vice president] Dick Cheney is captive to the Saudi Arabians. The real problem is the Israeli lobby on the grassy knoll, or dispensationalists covering up the Da Vinci code.

But all this is a conspiracy against the obvious. Perhaps many Americans actually prefer Israel's flawed democracy to the aging autocrats and corrupt monarchies of the region. Perhaps they root for a reliable ally that is surrounded by nations still committed to its destruction. Perhaps many Americans recall that the Jews, just six decades ago, lost one-third of their number to genocide and believe that this persecuted people deserves a secure home and sanctuary. Perhaps Americans understand that anti-Semitism was the greatest source of evil in the 20th century and is not dead in this one.

Walt and Mearsheimer are careful to say they are not anti-Semitic or conspiracy-minded. But their main inference—that Israel, the Israel lobby and Jewish neoconservatives called the shots for Bush, Cheney, [national security adviser, then secretary of state] Condoleezza Rice, [national security adviser] Stephen Hadley, [secretary of state] Colin Powell and [defense secretary] Donald Rumsfeld—is not only rubbish, it is dangerous rubbish. As "mainstream" scholars, Walt and Mearsheimer cannot avoid the historical pedigree of this kind of charge. Every generation has seen accusations that Jews have dual loyalties, promote war and secretly control political structures.

These academics may not follow their claims all the way to anti-Semitism. But this is the way it begins. This is the way it always begins.

> "We ... owe a debt of gratitude to our
> more virulent critics, whose efforts to
> ... portray us as anti-Semites merely
> confirmed many of our key points."

Did 'the Israel Lobby' Change Anything?

Stephen M. Walt

*Stephen M. Walt is an American professor of international af-
fairs at Harvard University's John F. Kennedy School of Government. In the following viewpoint, he reflects on the impact of his
book* The Israel Lobby *that he coauthored with John Mearsheimer. The book argues that pro-Zionist groups such as the American Israel Public Affairs Committee (AIPAC) lobby pushed
Americans to adopt anti-Palestinian policies in the Middle East.
Some accuse the book of being anti-Semitic, but Walt strongly
rejects such claims. Instead, he says recognizing the Israel lobby's
influence and combating it is the best way to support Israel and
America.*

As you read, consider the following questions:

1. Why does Walt say he owes a debt of gratitude to his
   more virulent critics?

2. What events does the author say helped inspire the creation of pro-Israel groups favoring smarter policies?

3. Why does Walt say that he does not regret writing his book?

Five years ago this week, John Mearsheimer and I published *The Israel Lobby* in the *London Review of Books*. Our goal in writing the article (and subsequent book) was to break the taboo on discussions of the lobby's impact on U.S. foreign policy and to transform it into a topic that people could talk about openly and calmly. Because we believed the "special relationship" that the lobby had promoted was harmful to the United States and Israel (not to mention the Palestinians), we hoped that a more open discourse on this topic would move U.S. Middle East policy in a direction that would be better for almost everyone.

Did we succeed?

There's little question that the article and book opened up discussion, aided by the efforts of a number of other people and by developments in the region (alas, most of them unfortunate). We also owe a debt of gratitude to our more virulent critics, whose efforts to misrepresent our work and portray us as anti-Semites merely confirmed many of our key points. We weren't surprised by these responses, but it was disappointing to see so much of the initial discussion focus on these bogus charges, instead of our actual arguments.

Yet despite these distractions, discussions of the lobby and its impact have moved from the fringes of U.S. discourse to the mainstream. Today, one can read or watch people from Jon Stewart to Andrew Sullivan to Glenn Greenwald to David Remnick to Nicholas Kristof acknowledging the lobby's role in shaping U.S. Middle East policy. Editorials in mainstream papers like the *New York Times* or the *Los Angeles Times* call for the U.S. government to adopt a tougher approach toward the Israeli government. More and more news stories on U.S.

Middle East policy refer to the "Israel lobby" as a serious political force, and not always in flattering terms. Even hard-line neoconservatives like David Frum now acknowledge the power of groups in the lobby, as in Frum's recent complaint that Sarah Palin failed to appreciate the political benefits she could gain by choosing to visit Israel under the auspices of the Republican Jewish Coalition, instead of going on her own. Of course, our book and article are surely not the only reason for this shift in discourse, but we probably played a role.

When we wrote the book, we also hoped that our work would provoke some soul-searching among "pro-Israel" individuals and groups in the United States, and especially those found in the American Jewish community. Why? Because interest-group politics are central to American democracy, and the most obvious way to shift U.S. policy on this issue would be to alter the attitudes and behavior of the interest groups that care most about it and exert the greatest influence over U.S. behavior.

Indeed, we explicitly said in the book that what was needed was a "new Israel lobby," one that would advocate policies that were actually in Israel's long-term interest (and would be more aligned with U.S. interests too). The problem, we emphasized repeatedly, was not the *existence* of a powerful interest group focused on these issues; the problem was that it was dominated by individuals and organizations whose policy preferences were wrongheaded. A powerful "pro-Israel" interest group that favored smart policies would be wholly desirable.

It is therefore gratifying to observe the emergence of J Street, to see groups like Americans for Peace Now and Jewish Voice for Peace become more vocal, and to see writers like Peter Beinart and David Remnick take public stances that are substantially different from ones they might have expressed a few years ago.

Two Israels

What we should call the West Bank is "nondemocratic Israel." The phrase suggests that there are today two Israels: a flawed but genuine democracy within the green line [that separates Israel and the Palestinians] and an ethnically based nondemocracy beyond it. It counters efforts by Israel's leaders to use the legitimacy of democratic Israel to legitimize the occupation and by Israel's adversaries to use the illegitimacy of the occupation to delegitimize democratic Israel. Having made that rhetorical divide, American Jews should look for every way possible to reinforce it. We should lobby the U.S. government to exempt settler goods [that is, goods made by Israelis settling in Palestinian territory] from its free-trade deal with Israel. We should push to end IRS [Internal Revenue Service] policies that allow Americans to make tax-deductible gifts to charities that fund settlements. We should urge the U.S. government to require Israel to separately mark products from the settlements, as the European Union now demands. Then we should stop buying those products and stop investing in the companies that produce them. Every time Avigdor Lieberman [an Israeli politician who has strongly supported settlements] or any other prominent public figure from nondemocratic Israel comes to the United States, he should be met with pickets. Every time any American newspaper calls Israel a democracy, we should urge that it include the caveat: only within the green line.

Peter Beinart,
The Crisis of Zionism, *2012.*

Needless to say, these shifts weren't our doing. Events in the region—especially the 2006 Lebanon war of 2006, the

2008–2009 Gaza war, the continued expansion of Israeli settlements, and the worrisome rightward drift in Israeli domestic politics—also inspired the effort to create a "pro-Israel" organization that would favor smarter policies and be more representative of American Jewish opinion than hard-line groups like AIPAC, the Israel Project, or the Zionist Organization of America, to say nothing of Christian Zionist organizations like John Hagee's Christians United for Israel.

Our greatest disappointment, however, has been the lack of movement in U.S. Middle East policy. On the one hand, Barack Obama's administration has resisted the lobby's pressure for military action against Iran, and it took office proclaiming its intention to achieve a two-state solution during Obama's first term. But on the other hand, Obama and his Middle East team have been unable or unwilling to act as an evenhanded mediator.

This situation is disappointing but not surprising. U.S. foreign policy rarely turns on a dime, and a central pillar like the "special relationship" doesn't change just because two academics write a controversial article. We didn't expect groups like AIPAC to dry up and blow away just because we had cast a critical spotlight on their activities, and the mechanisms that these and other groups have used to influence Congress and the executive branch remain potent.

The result, unfortunately, is that a two-state solution that would secure Israel's long-term future is farther away than ever, and America's image in the region—which showed signs of improvement at the time of Obama's 2009 Cairo speech—remains parlous. And we are now witnessing a series of political upheavals in the Arab world that are likely to create governments that are far more sensitive to public sentiment than their predecessors were, even if they fall short of being perfect democracies. These new governments will pay more attention to the "Arab street," where the Palestinian issue resonates in powerful ways. This situation will raise the costs of the "special relationship" even more, which makes America's failure to achieve a two-state solution over the past 20 years—a failure for which the lobby bears considerable (though not all) responsibility—especially tragic.

Finally, I am sometimes asked whether I have any regrets about writing the article or the book. My answer is clear: absolutely not. As I told a Harvard official back in 2006, it was a "life-altering" event in the sense that it almost certainly closed some doors that might otherwise have been open to me. But writing the book and engaging in serious public debate about Israeli policy, the "special relationship," and the lobby also taught me a lot about politics and introduced me to a new community of scholars, policy analysts, and journalists from whom I've learned an enormous amount and who have become valued colleagues. I would do it again without hesitation, and I would not alter any of our central arguments.

> *"Israel Firster' has a nasty anti-Semitic pedigree."*

Sounding Off

Spencer Ackerman

Spencer Ackerman is a journalist and blogger who writes for Wired. *In the following viewpoint, he argues that the term* Israel Firster *is an anti-Semitic smear. He says that those on the left have used the smear to suggest that right-wing American supporters of Israel are un-American and are not loyal to the United States. Ackerman argues that the term has an anti-Semitic history and has been used in the past to suggest that Jews are foreigners and disloyal. While Ackerman believes that the left's policy proposals are better for the United States and Israel, he contends that anti-Semitic slurs have no place in the debate.*

As you read, consider the following questions:

1. Who is Jeffrey Goldberg and how, according to Ackerman, was his loyalty questioned?

2. What is the Center for American Progress, and what, according to the author, is its role in the debate over the use of *Israel Firster*?

3. Why does Ackerman say that the left will win a debate about Israel policy on merits?

At the risk of sounding like the shtetl police, there's a right way and a wrong way for American Jews to argue with one another. The right way focuses on whose ideas are better—for America, for Israel, for the Jewish community, and for the world. The Jewish left should be right at home with this kind of substantive debate, since I believe those ideas are better than those of our cousins on the Jewish right. But the wrong way, regretfully, is now on the rise among Jewish progressives.

Some on the left have recently taken to using the term "Israel Firster" and similar rhetoric to suggest that some conservative American Jewish reporters, pundits, and policymakers are more concerned with the interests of the Jewish state than those of the United States. Last week, for example, Salon's Glenn Greenwald asked Atlantic writer Jeffrey Goldberg about any loyalty oaths to Israel Goldberg took when he served in the IDF during the early 1990s. (On Tuesday, writer Max Blumenthal used a gross phrase to describe Goldberg: "former Israeli prison guard.") The obvious implication is that Goldberg's true loyalty is to Israel, not the United States. For months, M.J. Rosenberg of Media Matters, the progressive media watchdog group, has been throwing around the term "Israel Firster" to describe conservatives he disagrees with. One recent Tweet singled out my friend Eli Lake, a reporter for Newsweek: "Lake supports #Israel line 100% of the time, always Israel first over U.S." That's quite mild compared to some of the others.

"Israel Firster" has a nasty anti-Semitic pedigree, one that many Jews will intuitively understand without knowing its specific history. It turns out white supremacist Willis Carto was reportedly the first to use it, and David Duke popularized it through his propaganda network. And yet Rosenberg and others actually claim they're using it to stimulate "debate," rather than effectively mirroring the tactics of some of the people they criticize.

Throughout my career, I've been associated with the Jewish left—I was to the left of the *New Republic* staff when I worked there, moved on to [the left-wing website] *Talking Points Memo*, hosted my blog at *Firedoglake* for years, and so on. I've criticized the American Jewish right's myopic, destructive, tribal conception of what it means to love Israel. But it doesn't deserve to have its Americanness and patriotism questioned. By all means, get into it with people who interpret every disagreement Washington has with Tel Aviv as hostility to the Jewish state. But if you can't do it without sounding like Pat Buchanan, who has nothing but antipathy and contempt for Jews, then you've lost the debate.

This is tiresome to point out. Many of the writers who are fond of the Israel Firster smear are—appropriately—very good at hearing and analyzing dog whistles when they're used to dehumanize Arabs and Muslims. I can't read anyone's mind or judge anyone's intention, but by the sound of it these writers are sending out comparable dog-whistles about Jews.

A bit of background for the uninitiated: Last month, Josh Block, a former AIPAC spokesman, pushed a series of talking points that targeted several liberal writers at the Center for American Progress [CAP], a left-wing think tank with ties to the Obama Administration. (Full disclosure: My personal blog was very briefly hosted by CAP in 2008; some of Block's targets are my friends.) The effect was to suggest that CAP was hostile to Israel because it is to Block's left. A plain reading of the think tank's work refutes the accusation.

But buried in Block's overbroad invective was a kernel of truth. Some at CAP, the liberal watchdog group Media Matters, and beyond deployed the "Israel First" smear, calling the Americanness of their political opponents into question. Predictably, right-wing Jewish writers took their shots at CAP,

A Jewish Pentagon Official Is Branded an *Israel Firster*

Hugh Hewitt: Now I've got to ask a tough, sensitive question here. Were you suspect because you are Jewish?

Douglas Feith [Pentagon official during the George W. Bush Administration who supports a US-Israeli military alliance]: Well, there have been some people who have made some very bigoted comments, attacking me and my motivation on the grounds that I'm Jewish, and have a long history of writing about Arab-Israeli issues, and writing in support of Israel. And people have made completely groundless, and I think really foul allegations that my motivation in working on all these things was not to serve the United States, but to serve Israel.

[Hewitt]: And I think that is really one of the worst things that can be said, and a terrible insult. But I'm actually going to a more sophisticated point, not the naked anti-Semites, or even the close to naked anti-Semites. But [in your book *War and Decision*] you write, "State Department officials would often comment on these issues by arguing that nothing of importance could be done to push back against jihadist extremism until we resolve terrorism's root causes." And of course, that always means the Palestinian-Israeli war. And I just get the sense that for some people, they can't see the world because they're focused on this one issue in the war, Israel-Palestine, and that anyone who wants to talk on other than that immediately gets branded as an Israel firster. It just seems to me a disease in the State Department.

Hugh Hewitt,
The War Against the West, *2008.*

Media Matters, and the rest—never wanting to miss an opportunity to indict the left. And the *Washington Post* revived the contretemps last month in an article that effectively asked if CAP was anti-Israel.

The response to this controversy, and related ones, was ugly. Many toyed with the idea that denigrating someone's American identity wasn't so bad after all. Left-wing polemicist Philip Weiss wrote that he considered the term "Israel firster [to be] a perfectly legitimate term in a wide-open American discourse." *Time* columnist Joe Klein noted that he's used the term himself before, weighing in on "Americans who are pushing for war with Iran"—as the question of attacking Iran lurks in the background of this entire debate;[1]—and who "place Israel's national defense priorities above our own."

Even more disappointingly, the term got a nod of approval from the head of a lobbying organization that represents the Jewish left. Jeremy Ben-Ami of J Street, the liberal, pro-Israel, pro-peace organization that I've written favorably about, told the *Washington Post* he was cool with the throwing of "Israel Firster" around. "If the charge is that you're putting the interests of another country before the interests of the United States in the way you would advocate that," he said, "it's a legitimate question." So, Ben-Ami's response to years of getting baselessly attacked for not caring about Israel is to turn around and say his attackers don't care about America? (Ben-Ami later clarified that, "The conspiracy theory that American Jews have dual loyalty is just that, a conspiracy theory and must be refuted in the strongest possible way.")

If what Rosenberg and the others on the left want is a debate—by which I understand them to mean a debate about the wisdom of a war with Iran, and about the proper role of the U.S.-Israel relationship—great. The left, I think, will win that debate on the merits, because it recognizes that if Israel is

---

1. Some on the right in Israel and America argue that Iran is developing nuclear weapons, and should be attacked before it can use them against Israel.

to survive as a Jewish democracy living in peace beside a free Palestine, an assertive United States has to pressure a recalcitrant Israel to come to its senses, especially about the insanity of attacking Iran.

But that debate will be shut down and sidetracked by using a term that Charles Lindbergh or Pat Buchanan would be comfortable using. I can't co-sign that. The attempt to kosherize "Israel Firster" is an ugly rationalization. It shouldn't matter that the American Jewish right proliferates the term "anti-Israel." The easiest way to lose a winnable argument is to get baited into using their tactics. I don't fetishize false civility; bullies ought to get it twice as bad as they give. People disagree, so they should argue. Shouting is healthier than shutting up.

Call me a squish or a sellout or a concern troll. Whatever. But if you can't be forceful without recalling some of the ugliest tropes in American Jewish history, you're doing it wrong.

| "*Israel Firster' is a perfectly legitimate term . . . [with] a long and honorable pedigree.*"

The Term *Israel Firster* Is Not an Anti-Semitic Slur

Philip Weiss

Philip Weiss is the founder and coeditor of Mondoweiss, an on-line forum on US politics and Mideast issues. In the following viewpoint, he argues that the term Israel firster *is not anti-Semitic but rather gets at an important issue in the relationship between the United States and Israel. He says that a Jewish state and Zionism (or Jewish nationalism) can create divided loyalties for American Jews. He points to declarations of loyalty to Israel by some American Jews and to the statements of early Zionists, who acknowledged the problem of dual loyalty. He concludes that the charge of anti-Semitism is just a way to close down an important conversation, and that* Israel firster *should still be used.*

As you read, consider the following questions:

1. According to Weiss, what evidence did Senator Chuck Schumer give of loyalty to Israel?

2. Why does Eric Alterman, as cited by the author, say that in some cases he may support what's best for Israel rather than what is best for the United States?

3. Who was Theodor Herzl, and where, according to Weiss, does he talk about the problem of dual loyalties among Jews?

The new battleground in the argument over Israel's influence on American policy is the idea that some of those pushing an attack on Iran are "Israel Firsters."

The term has been used by MJ Rosenberg of Media Matters and Zaid Jilani, formerly of the Center for American Progress. Israel supporters have struck back hard. They claim that using the term is anti-Semitic because it calls on a long history of questioning Jews' loyalty to western countries.

Yesterday Jeremy Ben-Ami of J Street bravely defended the use of the expression in an interview with the *Washington Post*. "If the charge is that you're putting the interests of another country before the interests of the United States in the way you would advocate that, it's a legitimate question," Ben-Ami said. (And today Ben-Ami, evidently summoned by commisar Jeffrey Goldberg, apologizes for misspeaking.)

I think "Israel firster" is a perfectly legitimate term in a wide-open American discourse—especially a debate about attacking another country. Obviously, it's loaded. It's a comment on a person's motivation, and it can be wielded as a form of redbaiting [denouncing someone as a Communist]. But as an intellectual and political question, it has a long and honorable pedigree.

Its legitimacy can be demonstrated by three factual arguments:

1, Israel supporters routinely make frank professions of loyalty that raise the issue. 2, Students of US policy, including many mainstream (and Jewish) writers, have blurted frank comments in recent years about dual loyalty, so it must be a useful term. 3, It was useful historically for three important theorists of Zionism [the belief in the need for a Jewish state], [Austrian journalist and father of Zionism] Theodor Herzl, [political theorist] Hannah Arendt, and [anti-Zionist] Rabbi Elmer Berger. If they get to talk about it, why can't we?

1). Public declarations of loyalty. Senator Chuck Schumer went to AIPAC [the American Israel Public Affairs Committee] and declared that his name means guardian in Hebrew and then he cried, "Am Yisroel Chai." The people of Israel live! MJ Rosenberg caught this:

> Schumer: "I believe Hashem [Orthodox for God] actually gave me that name. One of my roles, very important in the United States Senate, is to be a shomer [a Jewish legal guardian]—to be a, or the, shomer Yisrael. And I will continue to be that with every bone in my body. . ."

Loyalty to Israel

He's hardly alone. Neoconservative Elliott Abrams wrote in a book on Jewish identity that "outside the land of Israel, there can be no doubt that Jews, faithful to the covenant between God and Abraham, are to stand apart from the nation in which they live." Alan Dershowitz has written that American Jews have a "sacred mission" to protect Jewish lives in Israel, and [the American Jewish newspaper] *The Forward* has lately stated that Jewish university presidents have "loyalty" to Israel.

If all these folks can talk about their devotion to Israel, then why can't critics problematize that support and wonder if it crosses the line? Of course we can. That's called debate.

2. Lots of smart writers find the term useful. Before MJ Rosenberg and Zaid Jilani were attacked for talking about Israel firsters—and before Jilani apologized for doing so—many writers have questioned the allegiances of Israel supporters.

Joe Klein at *Time*:

> The fact that a great many Jewish neoconservatives—people like [Connecticut senator] Joe Lieberman and the crowd

over at *Commentary* [magazine]—plumped for this [Iraq] war, and now for an even more foolish assault on Iran, raised the question of divided loyalties: using U.S. military power, U.S. lives and money, to make the world safe for Israel.

John Judis, at the *New Republic*:

[Jewish leaders] want to demand of American Jewish intellectuals a certain loyalty to Israel, Israeli policies, and to Zionism as part of their being Jewish. They make dual loyalty an inescapable part of being Jewish in a world in which a Jewish state exists.

Eric Alterman of the *Nation* (speaking at the 92d St. Y [in New York City]):

I am a dual loyal Jew and sometimes I'm going to actually go with Israel, because the United States can take an awful lot of hits and come up standing. Whereas if Israel takes one serious bad hit it could disappear. So there's going to be some cases where when Israel and the United States conflict I'm going to support what's best for Israel rather than what I think is best for the United States. The big fiction that permeates virtually all discussion, and I bet you even in J Street, but certainly amongst official organizations, is that there's no such thing, that there could be possibly anything that could be both Good for Israel and Bad for the United States or vice versa.

A Secret Flag

Finally, culture critic Douglas Rushkoff has written that American Jewish confusion about which is our nation, epitomized by the two flags in the synagogue—"So the Jewish flag was our real flag—our secret flag—and the American flag was our conspicuous nod to the nation that we called home"—helped to produce the "compromise of Jewish ideals" that American Jewish support for Israel has involved.

3. *This problem was anticipated historically by leading theorists of Zionism.* The very best understanding of dual loyalty was expressed by Hannah Arendt, in 1944, when she said that if the creation *and long-term preservation* of a Jewish state depended upon American Jews, the relationship would foster questions of dual loyalty.

From *Zionism Reconsidered*:

> If a Jewish commonwealth is obtained in the near future ...
> it will be due to the political influence of American Jews.
> This would not need to affect their status of American citizenship if their "homeland" or "mother country" were a politically autonomous entity in a normal sense, or if their
> help were likely to be only temporary. But if the Jewish
> commonwealth is proclaimed against the will of the Arabs
> and without the support of the Mediterranean peoples, not
> only financial help but political support will be necessary
> for a long time to come. And that may turn out to be very
> troublesome indeed for Jews in this country [the United
> States]. .... It may eventually be far more of a responsibility
> than today they imagine or tomorrow can make good.

This is visionary, utterly visionary. Arendt anticipates the edifice of the Israel lobby [in the United States] in 2012. She anticipates Schumer declaring himself Israel's "guardian" in Hebrew, Eric Alterman saying that the U.S. can take some hits for Israel, Joe Klein wondering about the neocons' motivation for the Iraq war, and John Judis's understanding that dual loyalty is an "inescapable" part of American Jewish leadership.

Herzl and Loyalty

Now to Theodor Herzl, the founder of political Zionism. Herzl repeatedly refers to allegations of dual loyalty in his diaries chronicling his campaign for Zionism in the eight years before his death in 1904.

Herzl wanted to characterize these allegations as anti-Semitic—as dark questions that anti-Semites raise about good

Jews. But his diaries show that leading Jews, including the *Zionist Edmond de Rothschild, who was then paying for Jewish settlement in Palestine*, were concerned about the doubts posed to their patriotism by the foundation of a Jewish state.

From the diaries:

Paris. Nov. 10, 1895. Meeting with French Chief Rabbi Zadok Kahn.

He too professed himself to be a Zionist. But French "patriotism" also has its claims. Yes, a man has to choose between Zion and France.

Paris. Nov. 17, 1895. Meeting with Narcisse Leven, Jewish French leader.

When he harped on his French nationality I said, "What? Do not you and I belong to the same nation?"

London. Nov. 24, 1895. Meeting with Samuel Montagu, Member of Parliament.

He confessed to me—in confidence—that he felt himself to be more an Israelite than an Englishman.

May 1896, diary entry containing a report of the feelings of Edmond de Rothschild, a French banker and Zionist:

What I am doing he considers dangerous, because I render the patriotism of the Jews suspect.. . . .

The term "Israel Firster" gets at an inconvenient truth of Zionism: that when you establish a Jewish nation, it may raise questions about the interests of Jews outside the "homeland." Especially when they are pushing war that will help Israel.

Yes, some people who use the term may be anti-Semites. Yes, the term can be ugly. Just as the expression "the 1 percent" can be ugly if wielded crudely.

But smearing people who use the term "Israel firster" as anti-Semites is a very old Zionist tactic—because they don't want us to talk about a legitimate question, in this case whether an attack on Iran [which some supporters of Israel fear may be developing nuclear weapons with which to attack Israel] is in Americans' interests. As Arendt wrote:

> [W]hen the assimilationists talked about the danger of double loyalty and the impossibility of being German or French patriots and Zionists at the same time, they rudely raised a problem which for obvious reasons the Zionists did not care to talk of frankly.

Zionists have controlled the terms of this conversation for too long. The smearing of smart journalists as anti-Semites is yet another effort to do so.

Periodical and Internet Sources Bibliography

The following articles have been selected to supplement the diverse views presented in this chapter.

Abraham Foxman	"Anti-Zionism and Anti-Semitism," *In the News* (blog), *Jerusalem Post*, April 4, 2012. http://blogs.jpost.com/content/revisiting-anti-zionism-and-anti-semitism.
Emily L. Hauser	"Let's Talk About the Israel Lobby," *Emily L. Hauser—In My Head* (blog), September 14, 2012. http://emilylhauserinmyhead.wordpress.com/2012/09/14/lets-talk-about-the-israel-lobby.
Robert D. Kaplan	"Why John J. Mearsheimer Is Right (About Some Things)," *Atlantic Monthly*, January–February 2012.
Adam Kirsch	"Framed," *Tablet*, January 18, 2012. www.tabletmag.com/jewish-arts-and-culture/books/88397/framed-2.
Sarah Posner	"Is 'Israel-Firster' Anti-Semitic?," Religion Dispatches, March 6, 2012. www.religiondispatches.org/dispatches/sarahposner/5765/is_%22israel-firster%22_anti-semitic.
James Stern-Weiner	"Both Sides Are Wrong in the 'Israel Firsters' Debate," Mondoweiss, February 3, 2012. http://mondoweiss.net/2012/02/both-sides-are-wrong-in-the-israel-firsters-debate.html.
Stephen M. Walt	"How (Not) to Hide the Elephant in the Room," *Foreign Policy*, September 20, 2012. http://walt.foreignpolicy.com/posts/2012/09/20/how_not_to_hide_the_elephant_in_the_room.

CHAPTER 4

What Political Groups Are Linked to Anti-Semitism?

Chapter Preface

In Germany, male circumcision has become a controversial political issue. Jews and Muslims both circumcise male infants, which involves cutting a small bit of skin (the foreskin) from the penis. In 2012, a court in Cologne, Germany, ruled that male circumcision is harmful to infants and declared it illegal.

Opposition to circumcision is widespread in Germany—in one survey, 60 percent of respondents equated it with genital mutilation, according to a January 7, 2013, article by Joshua Hammer in the *Atlantic Monthly*. Hammer also suggests that the opposition to circumcision in Germany may be in part linked to anti-Semitism. Hammer points to Michael Schmidt-Salomon, an anti-circumcision activist whose 2008 children's book *How Do I Get to God, Asked the Small Piglet*, was condemned by German authorities for caricatures of religious figures, including one of a rabbi that some critics compared to Nazi propaganda. Brendan O'Neill in a June 28, 2012, article in the London *Telegraph* notes that "many anti-Jewish pogroms in the past were justified on the basis that Jews abused children" and concludes that the anti-circumcision advocates are demonizing Jews and people of faith.

Circumcision bans have also been attempted in the United States. In 2011, for example, activists in San Francisco attempted to pass a ballot measure making circumcision illegal, according to Carla Marinucci, writing in a June 3, 2011, post at SFGate, the online presence of the *San Francisco Chronicle*. Matthew Hess, a supporter of the ban, created a comic book featuring a blonde hero named "Foreskin Man" who fights "Monster Mohel"—a mohel being the rabbi who performs a circumcision. Blogger Andrew Sullivan, an outspoken opponent of male circumcision, found the comic so clearly offensive and anti-Semitic that he said that he had to oppose the

San Francisco ban. "One day, a rational, calm and tolerant campaign to prevent the routine mutilation of male infants will emerge," he said in a June 5, 2011, post. "But not this one. It's despicable."

As Sullivan indicates, not all opposition to circumcision is, or has to be, anti-Semitic. In fact, a number of Jewish groups and individuals have opposed circumcision at various points. Maayan Lubell in a November 28, 2012, article for Reuters news service reports that a growing number of Israeli Jews are choosing not to have their children circumcised. In the US, the group "Jews Against Circumcision" identify themselves on their website as "a group of educated and enlightened Jews who realize that the barbaric, primitive, torturous, and mutilating practice of circumcision has no place in modern Judaism."

Just as political movements in favor of circumcision have raised concerns about anti-Jewish sentiment, so other political groups or causes have also been involved in debates about anti-Semitism. The viewpoints in the following chapter examine several of these controversies.

| "There is a disturbing undercurrent to the current Occupy Wall Street movement. . . . It's anti-Semitism."

The Occupy Wall Street Movement Is Anti-Semitic

Ben Shapiro

Ben Shapiro is an American conservative political commentator, radio talk-show host, attorney, and media consultant. In the following viewpoint, he argues that the Occupy Wall Street (OWS) movement, which was formed to protest Wall Street's involvement in the 2008 financial collapse, is anti-Semitic. He points to statements and placards from OWS protesters that link capitalism to Judaism and to Israel. He says that such statements are similar to long-standing conspiracy theories about Jews controlling the world. He urges all politicians, and especially President Barack Obama, to repudiate OWS and its anti-Semitic message.

As you read, consider the following questions:

1. According to Shapiro, what anti-Semitic or anti-Israeli causes has President Obama been associated with besides Occupy Wall Street?

2. Who does the author identify as the nationalist hard left, and who does he identify as the internationalist hard left?

3. Why does Shapiro believe it may be hard for OWS to root out anti-Semitism?

There is a disturbing undercurrent to the current Occupy Wall Street [OWS] movement. It isn't merely its passionate denunciations of capitalism and excuses for corporatism. It isn't merely its perverse love for a president [Barack Obama] who has received more Wall Street money than any candidate in American history, and its hatred for Wall Street itself.

It's anti-Semitism.

Obama and Occupy Wall Street

Even as President Obama comes out in support of Occupy Wall Street, more and more Occupy rallies are laced with anti-Semitic signs, placards, and slogans. In New York, ralliers hold signs reading, "Google: (1) Wall Street Jews; (2) Jewish Billionaires; (3) Jews & Fed Rsrv Bank," "Gaza Supports the Occupation of Wall Street," and shouting ugly canards [lies] like "Jews control Wall Street." The American Nazi Party is supporting OWS, with leader Rocky Suhayda stating, "Who holds the wealth and power in this country—the Judeo-Capitalists. Who is therefore the #1 enemy who makes all this filth happen—the Judeo-Capitalists."

Not everyone occupying Wall Street is an anti-Semite. But there is far too high a comfort level among those in the movement for anti-Semitism. If the Tea Party [a right-wing Republican movement] had been even one tenth as laced with racism as the OWS movement is with anti-Semitism, it would have been put out of business by the mainstream press long ago.

The OWS' complacency with regard to anti-Semitism in its midst finds a mirror in the White House. President Obama

The Anti-Semitism of the Left

Because classical anti-Semitism was usually associated with the Right, the Left enjoyed a kind of bonus or free ride on matters relating to Jews and Israel. Unlike the Right, the Left could take the liberty of being anti-Israeli and (in part) even anti-Semitic. This bonus gave it the chance to establish an anti-Israeli discourse that has now become part of a widespread and accepted linguistic usage. Because of its general acceptability and legitimacy, left-wing criticism of Israel and left-wing anti-Semitism are far more relevant and alarming than what one finds on the Right, which has barely changed over the years. Today's neo-Nazis are ugly and unpleasant, and they continue to remain well beyond the bounds of what is respectable in the European discourse. The Left's anti-Semitism does not usually break clear [of] universally recognisable taboos. Left anti-Semitism does not often talk about world Jewish conspiracy and the *Protocols of the Elders of Zion*; or Jews as Christ-killers; or Jews as bloodsuckers; or Jews as capitalists; or Jews as racial polluters; nor does it deny the Holocaust in a straightforward manner. Left anti-Semitism does not derive from a clear and conscious hatred of Jews. Rather, it emanates from a particular understanding of global imperialism and of the role of Israel, Zionism and Jews within this bigger picture, wherein the United States plays an absolutely central role.

Andrei S. Markovits,
"European Anti-Semitism and Anti-Americanism,"
in Brendon O'Connor, ed., Anti-Americanism, *2007.*

supports OWS wholeheartedly—and why shouldn't he? After attempting time and again to force Israel to the negotiating table with terrorists, after using [his chief of staff] Rahm Emanuel to threaten Israel into concessions by warning that the US would allow Iran to go nuclear, after backing anti-Semitic revolutionaries from Egypt to Libya, after making friends with notorious Jew-haters like Rashid Khalidi [an American historian of the Middle East] and Jeremiah Wright [Obama's former pastor]—why shouldn't Obama extend that open hand to the folks at Occupy Wall Street?

The question is not why the left supports the anti-Semitism at Occupy Wall Street. The question is why the left seems to support anti-Semitism across the globe.

"Blood-Sucking" Capitalists

The focus on Zionism at the OWS rallies is odd, to say the least. Why should a foreign state located some 5700 miles from New York have any part in the discussion about America's economy? The answer is simple at root: the hard left still buys into the discredited notions of *The Protocols of the Elders of Zion* [an anti-Semitic book from the early 20th century], in which Jews supposedly plotted the takeover of the world economy. Zionism, in this twisted vision, is the wellspring of that control—Jerusalem is supposedly the capital of the Jew/banker conspiracy. That sick notion pervades the rhetoric of the OWS rallies. Says one OWS rallier in Los Angeles, "I think the Zionist Jews who are running these big banks and our Federal Reserve . . . need to be run out of this country." Says another in Chicago, "Israel is beginning to be seen as the criminal pariah state that it is."

This nasty thought pattern unites both the nationalist and the internationalist hard left. The nationalist hard left—i.e. neo-Nazis and white supremacist groups, as well as many nationalist groups in Europe—see Israel as a façade for a globalist Jewish regime seeking to bring "blood-sucking" capitalism to prominence. The internationalist hard left—i.e. OWS and its ilk—see Israel as the last vestige of discredited nationalism, and Wall Street as its colonialist branch in the United States.

If OWS wants to be taken seriously as a movement, its members need to root out the anti-Semitism from their midst. Then again, that rooting out process may not be possible because of how close the cancer of anti-Semitism is to the heart of the movement. If that is the case, every responsible politician has the responsibility to disassociate from OWS. Somehow, in the case of the Obama administration, that seems unlikely, no matter how outrageous the Jew-hatred gets at OWS.

│ *"Anti-Semitism has not gained traction*
│ *... nor is it representative of the larger*
│ *[Occupy Wall Street] movement."*

Where Are the Anti-Semites of Occupy Wall Street?

Richard Cohen

Richard Cohen is a syndicated columnist for the Washington Post. *In the following viewpoint, he reports on visiting Occupy Wall Street rallies against Wall Street's role in the financial crisis on multiple occasions and finding no hint of anti-Semitism. In stead, he says, Jewish holidays were celebrated. He argues that Occupy Wall Street is largely irrelevant and aimless but strongly condemns the smear of anti-Semitism. He suggests the charge in this case is used merely to score political points rather than because of any real danger from anti-Jewish sentiment.*

As you read, consider the following questions:

1. What is the Anti-Defamation League's position on anti-Semitism in Occupy Wall Street, according to Cohen?

2. What aspect of Occupy Wall Street has made the right-wing's attempt to discredit it possible, according to the author?

3. What does Cohen say is to be done about the Occupy Wall Street controversy?

Reckless Jew that I am, I muscled my way into the Occupy Wall Street encampment in Lower Manhattan despite multiple reports of virulent and conceivably lethal anti-Semitism. Projecting an unvarnished Semitism, I circled the place, encountering nothing and no one to suggest bigotry—not a sign, not a book and not even the guy who some weeks ago held up a placard with the instruction to Google the phrase "Zionists control Wall St." Google "nutcase" instead.

Searching for Anti-Semites

This was my second visit to the Occupy Wall Street site and the second time my keen reporter's eye has failed to detect even a hint of the anti-Semitism that had been trumpeted by certain right-wing Web sites and bloggers, most prominently [neocon pundit] Bill Kristol. He is a founder of the Emergency Committee for Israel, which has been running cable TV ads alleging a virtual hate rally at the Occupy Wall Street site and calling on President [Barack] Obama and other important Democrats to denounce what is—as it happens—not happening there. The commercial ran on Fox News the very day I was at the site.

Kristol's *cri de wolf* (a French term of my own invention) was taken up by Jennifer Rubin, *The Washington Post*'s conservative blogger, who noted the Kristol group's "eye-popping ad." Citing an article from *Israel Today* that linked a single statement by someone named Patricia McAllister in Los Angeles with some vitriol on the American Nazi Party's Web site and a reference to the editor of *Adbusters*, she fashioned a veritable pogrom [systematic Jewish persecution] out of pretty close to thin air and demanded, "Where is the outrage?" I have a better question: Where are the anti-Semites?

The Anti-Defamation League has managed to find a paltry few. But even this watchdog Jewish organization, while noting the odd Jew-hater on the periphery of the anti–Wall Street group, found that "anti-Semitism has not gained traction . . . nor is it representative of the larger movement at this time." Possibly more representative is the fact that Jewish religious services were held at the protest site for the holidays of Yom Kippur and Simchat Torah. If these were disrupted by roving bands of contemporary Cossacks [an ethnic group in Russia associated with brutality and attacks on Jews], the local media have failed to mention it—yet another cause for outrage, no doubt.

This right-wing attempt to discredit both the Occupy Wall Street movement and the Democratic Party's hesitant embrace of it is reprehensible. It's made possible, however, because no one this side of the moon knows precisely what the Occupy Wall Street movement is trying to do. On a daily basis it marches off to some location to highlight what we all know— that Wall Street guys are rich—and their slogans suggest a tired socialism that is as repugnant to me as the felonious capitalism that produced the mortgage bubble and the impoverishment of millions of Americans [in the 2008 financial crisis]. Given our fastidiousness regarding vigilante justice, not much can be done.

A Vast Sleepover

Occupy Wall Street has become an event for its own sake, a destination for the aimless. It is something that occurs on countless iPhone cameras, a tourist attraction with the usual vendors, the usual zaftig [full-figured] young women doing the usual arrhythmic dance, somehow missing the beat of many drums. The nostalgic scent of pot wafts occasionally through the air, and I feel so much younger. This, I'm sure, will bring an end to the Vietnam War.

On a given day, I decide that Occupy Wall Street is about nothing and then I decide it is the Herman Cain[1] campaign in aggregate, just a media event that has captured the flea-thoughts of many Americans. Then I decide it is an incoherent articulation of anger at the institutions that have failed us, including—by way of both self-pity and self-flagellation—the media. It seems, above all, a conspiracy to have left-leaning writers make jackasses of themselves by imparting grave and grand meaning to what is little more than a vast sleepover.

The imputation of anti-Semitism, however, adds gravitas [weight, in the sense of importance] to this lighthearted event. The smear is in deadly earnest, a reminder that the devious tactics of the Old Left have been adopted by the New Right. (No accident, maybe, that the practitioners are the descendants of lefties.) It produced alarm on the Internet, Jewish smoke signals alerting the ethnically twitchy to the presence of enemies and the demand that Obama, already suspected of harboring furious anti-Israel sentiments, do something. But there is nothing to be done—except to condemn anyone who uses anti-Semitism to advance a political agenda. To quote some of them: Where's the outrage?

---

1. Herman Cain is a businessman who ran for the Republican presidential nomination in 2012 and enjoyed a brief celebrity.

> *"Should the rest of us be concerned when a white nationalist racist . . . appears at the same event as . . . Mitt Romney, Newt Gingrich, Rick Santorum and Sarah Palin?"*

US Conservatives Embrace White Nationalist Anti-Semites and Racists

Menachem Z. Rosensaft

Menachem Z. Rosensaft is the vice president of the American Gathering of Jewish Holocaust Survivors and Their Descendants. In the following viewpoint, Rosensaft reports that the influential Conservative Political Action Conference (CPAC), important within the Republican Party, invited Peter Brimelow to appear on a panel. Rosensaft argues that Brimelow is a white nationalist who has used his website to promote the views of white supremacists and anti-Semites. Rosensaft says that Republicans should repudiate Brimelow and those like him, and should distance themselves from the ideology of white supremacy.

As you read, consider the following questions:

1. How did the ADL say that Brimelow demonstrated his racist views, according to Rosensaft?

2. As reported by the author, where does the name VDARE.com come from?

3. What views of Kevin MacDonald caused the ADL to identify him as an anti-Semite, according to Rosensaft?

Reacting to the inclusion of the "white nationalist" anti-immigration activist Peter Brimelow on a panel on "The Failure of Multiculturalism: How the Pursuit of Diversity Is Weakening the American Identity" at this year's Conservative Political Action Conference (CPAC), Ed Schultz observed on MSNBC's *The Ed Show* that, "We've come to expect CPAC to bring together the far righties. But even CPAC should draw the line somewhere."

Schultz went on to quote Brimelow as having said at CPAC that, "Democrats have given up on winning the white working class vote, so they use bilingualism to build up a client constituency. It's treason. We hear about racism, but the real issue is treason."

Brimelow certainly doesn't mince words. He told a CBS reporter that US immigration policy, the legal kind, mind you, is creating a "Spanish speaking underclass parallel to the African American underclass."

"These are people who are completely dysfunctional," Brimelow said. "They're on welfare; they're not doing any kind of work—at least not legal work—and their children are having a terrible time." California, which used to be "paradise," he added, is "rapidly turning into a Hispanic slum."

Nice. So who, precisely, is Peter Brimelow, and why should the rest of us be concerned when a white nationalist racist like him appears at the same event as, say, Mitt Romney, Newt Gingrich, Rick Santorum and Sarah Palin?

Brimelow is founder and editor of the VDARE.com website which has been designated, a "hate group" by the Southern Poverty Law Center, and which, according to no less an authority than the Anti-Defamation League, "features the work of racists, anti-Semites and anti-immigrant figures."

The ADL has been following Brimelow's activities for some time. In February of 2009, the organization tells us, "Brimelow demonstrated his racist views" at "a conference of racists in Baltimore, Maryland, dedicated to 'Preserving Western Civilization.'" There, Brimelow "delivered one of the most extreme presentations at the conference. He argued that the influx of "non-traditional" immigration is a problem all over the Western world and that the loss of control over the country by "white Protestants" will mean a collapse of the American political system. He urged that whites respond by creating an explicitly white nationalist political party."

Hmm? An "explicitly white nationalist political party"? Where have we heard that before?

Here are some more of Brimelow's words of wisdom. In his 1995 book, *Alien Nation: Common Sense About America's Immigration Disaster*, he referred to the Clinton administration as a "black-Hispanic-Jewish-minority white (Southerners used to call them 'scalawags') coalition." The Merriam-Webster online dictionary, incidentally, defines a "scalawag" as a "a white Southerner acting in support of the reconstruction governments after the American Civil War often for private gain."

In an August 22, 2006, article, Brimelow called US immigration policy "Adolf Hitler's posthumous revenge on America." On February 15, 2011, he wrote that, "as immigration policy drives whites into a minority, this type of interest-group 'white nationalism' will inexorably increase."

In an October 6, 2009, article Brimelow wrote that, "it's still 'about race'. It is no coincidence, comrades, that the backlash is overwhelming white. Whites in America voted heavily against Obama. White Protestants ('let's face it, they are America'—Phillip Roth, *American Pastoral*, p. 311) still make up nearly half (42%) the electorate and they voted 2–1 for McCain. But are even 4% of Obama's appointments white Protestants?"

Following the 2008 presidential election, Brimelow told the H.L. Mencken Club in Baltimore, Maryland, that "McCain should have portrayed Obama as the affirmative-action candidate. It would have been so easy. All he had to do is get up and say it." President Obama, Brimelow went on, would eventually do something "that will start to shock people right away. I think that whites—that is to say, Americans—will organize."

Back in 2002, the conservative columnist Jonah Goldberg wrote in the *Los Angeles Times* that Brimelow, Pat Buchanan and Sam Francis "have become dismayingly obsessed in recent years with creating . . . an 'identity politics for white people.'" Goldberg described Brimelow as "a once-respected conservative voice who now runs the shrill anti-immigration website VDARE.com, named for Virginia Dare, the first British child born in North America." Goldberg also wrote that Buchanan's book, *The Death of the West* "warns hysterically that the white race is becoming an 'endangered species,' about to be swallowed up by the duskier Third World (defined as all nonwhites no matter how rich, educated or democratic)," and that Francis "has argued earnestly for 'imposing adequate fertility controls on nonwhites.'" Buchanan, Brimelow and Francis, Goldberg concluded, "live in denial about how to get back to the days when America was 90% white."

Brimelow claims that VDARE "will publish anyone, of any political tendency (or race), who has anything sensible to say about America's immigration disaster. And that certainly includes writers, for example Jared Taylor [see below], whom I would regard as 'white nationalist,' in the sense that they aim to defend the interests of American whites. They are not white supremacists. They do not advocate violence. They are rational and civil. They brush their teeth."

Kevin MacDonald and Anti-Semitic White Nationalism

For California State University, Long Beach, psychology professor Kevin MacDonald, an alleged white nationalist of the anti-Semitic stripe, Jews are a fundamental threat to white Americans. In MacDonald's view, Jews are essential to explaining the lack of an organized white movement. In a recent piece for the white nationalist journal *The Occidental Quarterly*, for which he serves as an editorial advisor, MacDonald (2006–2007) argued that whites "are better able to inhibit their relatively positive attitudes about their own group," causing them not to forge strong racial bonds with their fellow kinsmen. In effect, whites have the self-control to supersede their genetically driven biases for their own kind. However, according to MacDonald, this positive quality has left white people vulnerable. Taking advantage of this lack of strong racial bias, liberal activists in league with "a Jewish elite hostile to the traditional peoples and culture of Europe" have created what MacDonald calls a *culture of critique* that demonizes any expression of white identity and favors leftist, egalitarian ideas about race and ethnicity. This strategy has effectively permeated "intellectual and political discourse among both liberals and conservatives and define[d] a mainstream consensus among elites in academia, the media, business and government." The result is that white people have been prevented from developing a true consciousness of their own race. Hence, for MacDonald, the Jews are primarily responsible for impeding the healthy development of white nationalism.

Heidi Beirich and Kevin Hicks, "White Nationalism in America," in Barbara Perry et al., Hate Crimes, 2009.

Ok, then, here are some of the authors Brimelow has published on VDARE, and draw your own conclusions:

- Sam Francis who wrote on July 21, 2003, that: "America was defined—almost explicitly, sometimes very explicitly—as a white nation, for white people, and what that means is that there is virtually no figure, no law, no policy, no event in the history of the old, white America that can survive the transition to the new and non-white version. Whether we will want to call the new updated version 'America' at all is another question entirely."

- Kevin MacDonald, identified by the ADL as "anti-Semitic," who wrote on November 14, 2006, that: "Jewish activity collectively, throughout history, is best understood as an elaborate and highly successful group competitive strategy directed against neighboring peoples and host societies. The objective has been control of economic resources and political power. One example: overwhelming Jewish support for non-traditional immigration, which has the effect of weakening America's historic white majority."

- The same Kevin MacDonald wrote on November 5, 2005, in a review of *The Jewish Century* by one Yuri Slezkine that: "Despite the important role of Jews among the Bolsheviks, most Jews were not Bolsheviks before the Revolution. However, Jews were prominent among the Bolsheviks, and once the Revolution was underway, the vast majority of Russian Jews became sympathizers and active participants. . . . Slezkine's main point is that the most important factor for understanding the history of the 20th century is the rise of the Jews in the West and the Middle East, and their rise and decline in Russia. I think he is absolutely right about this. If there is any lesson to be learned, it is that

Jews not only became an elite in all these areas, they became a hostile elite—hostile to the traditional people and cultures of all three areas they came to dominate. . . . Given this record of Jews as a very successful but hostile elite, it is possible that the continued demographic and cultural dominance of Western European peoples will not be retained, either in Europe or the United States, without a decline in Jewish influence."

- Jared Taylor, who wrote on July 4, 2008, that: "What race realists find most infuriating about the liberalism of the last half century is not just that it has lost its instinctive appreciation for the culture and people of the West but actively, viciously attacks them. Whites are doing something no other people have ever done in human history. Our rulers and elites welcome replacement by aliens, they vilify our ancestors and their own, they sacrifice our interests to those of favored minorities, and they treat the entire history of the West as if it were a global plague of rapine and exploitation. This is a disease that is killing us, and we must fight it head on."

- The same Jared Taylor wrote on January 4, 2011, that: "Some of us, however, rather like being White, and would like for our children and grandchildren to be White too. The self-haters are welcome to go extinct if that is what they want. But what would be wrong in wanting a country—even a small country—where Whites are the majority and intend to keep it that way?"

After specifically referencing Peter Brimelow's "musings about racial dilution and the perils facing white people" on VDARE, a February 1, 2009, *New York Times* editorial observed that:

It is easy to mock white-supremacist views as pathetic and to assume that nativism in the age of Obama is on the way out. The country has, of course, made considerable progress since the days of Know-Nothings and the Klan. But racism has a nasty habit of never going away, no matter how much we may want it to, and thus the perpetual need for vigilance.

We all know that there are bigots amongst us who espouse theories of racial, ethnic or religious superiority. They have the right to express their views, however noxious, on street corners or on their websites. No one, however, is obliged to invite them to be part of polite society.

The fact that the organizers of CPAC chose to give Peter Brimelow a platform reflects on them. Why the other CPAC participants have chosen not to denounce or even distance themselves from his toxic rhetoric is a question well worth asking.

*"The subtle bigotry of some fellow liber-
als . . . violates the very humanitarian
rhetoric that gives it cover."*

American Liberals Are Guilty of Anti-Semitism

Valerie Tarico

Valerie Tarico is a psychologist and the author of The Dark
Side: How Evangelical Teachings Corrupt Love and Truth. *In
the following viewpoint, she argues that liberal anti-Semitism is
less violent and obvious than right-wing anti-Semitism but that
it is still powerful. In particular, she says that liberals tend to
single out Israel for particular censure, ignoring its difficult situation and also ignoring human rights abuses or failures by other
nations in the world. She says that focusing anger on Israel in
this way recalls a long history of antipathy towards Jews. She argues that liberals should focus less on Israel and more on reducing their own anti-Semitism.*

As you read, consider the following questions:

1. What Seattle experiences does Tarico refer to as evidence
   of anti-Semitism?

2. Why do Palestinians not leave Gaza and the West Bank, according to Tarico?

3. What brutalities in the world does Tarico specifically refer to as evidence that liberals tend to focus disproportionately on the Palestinians?

you filth jew liberil america hating jesus hating basterd Lord willing none of us will have to wait long america is too good for dirty jew scum of your family and your commie foundasion

—*anonymous email, April 21, 2009*

Mikey Weinstein is President and Founder of the Military Religious Freedom Foundation. A Jew, a former [Ronald] Reagan White House attorney and an honors graduate of the Air Force Academy in Colorado Springs, he spends his days fighting back against what has been called an "Evangelical coup" in the U.S. Military. Mikey writes letters, makes phone calls, lobbies and, when all else fails, files lawsuits on behalf of religious minorities and mainline Christians who are being subjected to relentless proselytizing from fundamentalist officers and peers. One routine part of the reaction is letters like the one he received above.

Liberals and Israel

Liberal anti-Semitism is more sophisticated and subtle. Even at our worst, we don't talk about Jews, we talk about 9/11 conspiracies orchestrated by agents of Mossad [the Israeli intelligence agency]. We talk, as our medieval Christian and Christian Nationalist predecessors did before us, about undue Jewish control of the monetary system. Mostly we talk about Zionists [Jewish nationalists], and every Jew who has a more complex perspective on the Middle East than [liberal radio host] Amy Goodman is one.

I'm not a Jew. I am a psychologist. One of the things I learned as a therapist was to respond not just to surface words but also to the feelings and implications behind them. As a therapist, you listen to your body, your intuitive response to what is being said, and then you use your mind to sort things out. I can't say how many comments about the Israel-Palestine situation I've read on left-of-center blogs. What I can say is that the comment threads often make my stomach hurt—and not because of what is going on in Israel and Palestine. . . .

Yes, the plight of the Palestinians is anguishing. And yes, Israel has violated international law and may well be guilty of war crimes. But at a visceral level I often have a hard time experiencing my own pain and moral sensibilities about the Middle East situation. I get so overwhelmed by the flood of thinly veiled Jew-loathing that I can't respond to anything else.

(Insertion: Let me state for the record: I categorically do not believe that criticizing Israel is inherently anti-semitic. There is plenty of reason to protest Israel's part in the seemingly endless Middle Eastern cycles of violence and suffering. What I am talking about is a certain quality of this conversation—a distancing from Israelis explicitly or Jews more broadly as people, an exceptionalism that characterizes liberal American disgust at and demands of Jews, a pattern of silence toward some things and outrage toward others that suggest bias. And subtle or not-so-subtle versions of traditional anti-Semitic stereotypes that escape criticism [except from offended Jews] on liberal blogs.)

Perhaps I am projecting my Seattle experiences onto the net. One sweet, progressive activist neighbor refused to come to a panel discussion I hosted because, along with an atheist, a Christian minister and a Sufi minister the panel included a rabbi. A friend equated the invasion of Gaza [by Israel in 2008–2009] with the Holocaust. A political teammate couldn't see the difference between *Obsession*'s bitter flow of misogynist verses and the forged conspiracies in the *The Protocols of the Elders of Zion* [an early twentieth-century anti-Semitic book]. (They do all love Amy Goodman.) So maybe my gut is wrong.

But besides gut feelings, there are other indicators that something more than compassion, fairness, and yearning for a better world is at play in our reaction to the plight of the Palestinians. Several writers have listed factors that in their minds differentiate legitimate criticism of Israel from antisemitism. Here are some things that caught my attention:

Legitimate and Illegitimate Criticism

1. *The failure to focus on the log in our own eye.* Two towers come down and 4000 people die, and the majority of our population (who suddenly feel unsafe) give their blessing to the destruction of 100,000 Iraqi citizens, their basic infrastructure, their museums and their schools. Yet we mock the Israelis' sense of threat and demand inhuman perfection in their reaction. Granted, American liberals have worked long and hard against war in Iraq, but we were more conflicted about Afghanistan. And in both cases the protests lacked the absolutism of our reactions to Israel. I hear the Israeli attack on Gaza described as genocide. I never hear the American attack on Iraq described that way.

2. *Our silence when it comes to the role of the surrounding countries, who want the Palestinians to remain right where they are as pawns in a global power struggle.* Palestinians don't have the option to leave because Syria, Jordan, Egypt, and others don't give them that option any more than we do. Israeli-Gaza border closures work only when Egypt keeps her border closed as well. Within any group of refugees there are those who don't want to sacrifice their children on the altar of their politics— who simply want to leave and start a better life. But

they are denied resettlement rights elsewhere. The Palestinian people are *bandilleras* (lances) in the flanks of a Spanish bull—goads that feed the pain and rage needed to sustain a battle of civilizations.

3. *Our indifference to Jewish post traumatic dynamics and conditions that reactivate trauma.* In Israel, men who spent their teenage years dragging bodies out of gas chambers and burying them in trenches are only just dying off. To make matters worse, threats of annihilation are ongoing. When a woman who has been molested has someone hit on her, she often gets triggered, under or over reacting because she is re-experiencing the earlier trauma. When people who have been the targets of genocide hear surrounding leaders pledge their extinction, I might imagine they would get triggered, too. If we Liberals are willing to assume that it takes a people generations to recover from slavery, can we not assume the same of genocide? I grieve at Israeli reactivity just as I grieve when African American young people say that success is White. But grieving and demanding that they be over it are two different things.

4. *A double standard for Middle Eastern countries.* When Arabs or Muslims engage in mass political extermination, we say little. The same with smaller cruelties. Yet we hold the Israelis to a higher standard. Why is this? Why do we scream about Israeli rockets and yet we're mum when Hamas and Fatah are murdering each other? How about the slaughter of the Kurds or on a smaller scale, the execution of female teachers in Afghanistan? Sometimes I wonder if it is actually a form of racism against Arabs and Muslims, like when we assume that a kid is fated to be a low-achiever and we write them off. But consider: How would we react if the Israelis treated their women like Saudis do? If they treated their Hindu

servants like Omanis do? If they treated their religious minorities like the Iraqis do? If they pledged the extermination of Palestinians the way that Hamas pledges itself to the extermination of Jews?

5. *Our lack of comparable passion about other suffering in the world.* How come the Palestinian plight taps deep feelings for so many liberals, and yet brutalities in Sudan or Sri Lanka don't have the same power to arouse us? To draw an analogy from my anti-fundamentalism work, when Evangelicals cite Leviticus to justify their attitudes toward homosexuals but then ignore the rest of Mosaic Law, something other than biblical literalism is at play. When the suffering of the Palestinian people arouses venom that seeps through in Liberal rants while other suffering leaves us cold, something other than compassion is at play.

Singling Out Jews

I loathe the kind of ignorant rant that kicked off this article. But the subtle bigotry of some fellow liberals feels worse. It violates the very humanitarian rhetoric that gives it cover. As a progressive, it shames me. And it makes me scared.

Christians and their cultural descendants have been finding reasons to single out Jews since the time of Paul. Always there is some social issue that makes the antipathy seem justified to many people in the short run. And always to date anti-Semitism seems obvious in retrospect.

We humans are probably hard-wired for tribalism, and we need little excuse to see the "other" as disgusting or evil. But we also are capable of thinking more complexly. One who suffered much, [Russian political prisoner and author] Aleksandr Solzhenitsyn, had this to say: "If only it were all so simple, if only there were evil people somewhere insidiously committing evil deeds and it were necessary only to separate them from the rest of us and destroy them. But the line dividing good and evil cuts through the heart of every human being." Maybe in addition to looking at the dividing lines in the Middle East we could be looking more at the dividing lines in our own hearts.

> *"The Hungarian Guard ... bears a striking resemblance to the Arrow Cross, the feared fascist party that rose to prominence in the 1930s and had strong ties to Hitler."*

Anti-Semitism Is Growing Among the European Right

Alex Pearlman

Alex Pearlman is a human rights journalist and blogger for Global Post. In the following viewpoint, he reports on the growth of nationalism, white supremacy, anti-Semitism, and anti-immigrant sentiment among the Far Right in Europe. He talks about the anti-Semitism in Hungary, deportations of Roma (aka gypsies) in France, the growth of a thuggish neo-Nazi immigrant-bashing party in Greece, and other developments. He suggests that Europe needs to confront these ugly incidents and that politicians should sanction and distance themselves from such rhetoric.

As you read, consider the following questions:

1. What was depicted in the anti-Semitic cartoon that Heinz-Christian Strache of Austria's far-right Freedom Party posted to his Facebook page, as related by Pearlman?

2. How has France bypassed court review of its deportation of Roma, according to Human Rights Watch, as cited by the author?

3. What is Golden Dawn, according to Pearlman?

A legislator from Hungary's far-right Jobbik party made headlines last week [in August 2012]. When he was dismissed from the party and pressured to quit his position in the EU [European Union] Parliament after news of his Jewish roots became public.

Csanad Szegedi's history of anti-Semitic rhetoric cemented his prominent place in Hungary's right wing, but now amid scandal, he says he wants to get in touch with his roots. He's spoken with a rabbi and says he wants to visit Auschwitz, according to the [London newspaper] *Independent*. Jobbik maintains his removal from the party has nothing to do with his Jewish heritage, and that he was punished for suspected bribery, which allegedly occurred when his Judaism was discovered and he attempted to pay people to cover it up.

Szegedi was also a founding member of the rabid paramilitary Nazi spin-off group, the Hungarian Guard, which was banned by the courts in 2009. It bears a striking resemblance to the Arrow Cross, the feared fascist party that rose to prominence in the 1930s and had strong ties to Hitler.

But Hungary isn't alone in its surging right wing. Here are five countries undergoing a rightist resurgence.

Austria Echoes Nazi Germany

The central European country [of Austria] generally stays off the world stage, but a cartoon posted on Facebook has shaken things up. The AP [Associated Press] reports that Heinz-Christian Strache, the leader of Austria's far-right Freedom Party [FPOe], posted an anti-Semitic cartoon which showed "an overweight man with a crooked nose and cufflinks with the Star of David in front of plates of food, while an emaciated man looked on. The fat man represented the banking system and his thin companion the people, according to the legend."

The cartoon is similar to those used in Nazi German newspapers in the 20th century, and the Jewish community has erupted in protest.

"It's not a coincidence that a caricature of Jews, like the ones in [the Nazi newspaper] 'Stuermer' in the 1930s and 1940s appeared on the Facebook page of FPOe leader Strache," prominent Jewish leader Oskar Deutsch said to AP.

But it gets worse. Strache also posted a picture of himself on his Facebook page standing next to a roast pig with the caption, "Isst du Schwein, darfst du rein," which translates to "If you eat pork, you can come in."

Representatives from the conservative People's Party, as well as the Green and Socialist parties have spoken out against the Freedom Party's anti-Semitic and Islamophobic lines, but so far Strache and the Freedom Party maintain the posts were innocent.

France Continues Roma Discrimination

We've written here about anti-Muslim sentiment in France, mostly to do with the controversial ban on burqas and other facial/head coverings. But besides the sweeping Islamophobia in the country, the Roma face a similar and brutal kind of discrimination in France. Human Rights Watch [HRW] and other organizations are concerned that France's methods of dealing with the Roma [often called gypsies] population violate EU and international rights laws.

Earlier this month [August 2012], and possibly throughout the summer (there are three known instances, according to *Reuters*), authorities have swept Roma camps around France, deporting Romanian and Bulgarian ethnic Roma back to their home countries through a "voluntary" process that includes

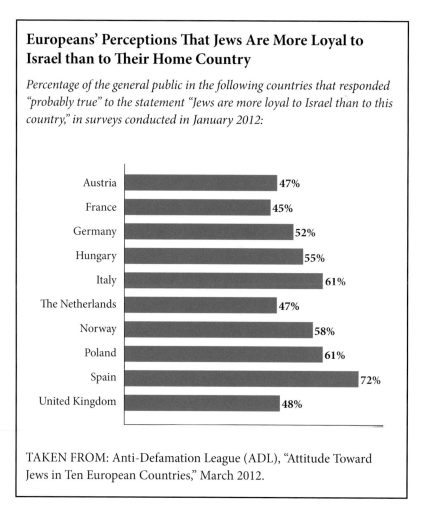

Europeans' Perceptions That Jews Are More Loyal to Israel than to Their Home Country

Percentage of the general public in the following countries that responded "probably true" to the statement "Jews are more loyal to Israel than to this country," in surveys conducted in January 2012:

Country	Percentage
Austria	47%
France	45%
Germany	52%
Hungary	55%
Italy	61%
The Netherlands	47%
Norway	58%
Poland	61%
Spain	72%
United Kingdom	48%

TAKEN FROM: Anti-Defamation League (ADL), "Attitude Toward Jews in Ten European Countries," March 2012.

paying 300 euros and a plane ticket. Because they leave "voluntarily," the eviction system "bypasses any court review of the removals," said HRW.

"This week's raids appear to be just the latest manifestation of France's notorious expulsion policy targeting Eastern European Roma," said Veronika Szente Goldston, Europe and Central Asia advocacy director at Human Rights Watch. "Rather than trying to get rid of unwanted Roma while no one is watching, the government should take a critical look at its sorry record in this area, and act to rectify abuses."

New President François Hollande is facing criticism for the continued removal of Roma and razing of camps, hallmarks of his predecessor, [Nicolas] Sarkozy. The anti-Roma movement by the administration is particularly alarming, especially considering Hollande's pre-election promise to end such discriminatory (and possibly highly illegal) practices by the French government.

"Hollande's promises to end discrimination against Roma couldn't ring more hollow in the wake of this week's events," Szente Goldston said on HRW's website. "Rather than embracing its predecessor's approach, the Hollande government should urgently fix France's problematic Roma expulsion policy."

In another time, the evacuation and relocation of Roma out of France might be called forced deportation, but the 300 euros is both an incentive to move and legal cover.

Xenophobia in Greece

Xenophobia and anti-immigrant sentiment has reached an alarming high in Greece this summer, capped by a victory by the far-right party Golden Dawn in the June elections, which came away with 18 parliamentary seats. Golden Dawn is known for its swastika-like symbol, a salute reminiscent of the Nazis, and a fan base of very serious nationalists.

A recent article in the *New York Times* and a report by Human Rights Watch explain that along with electoral momentum, Greece is seeing a wave of vigilante violence against immigrants.

The *New York Times* article opens:

A week after an extremist right-wing party gained an electoral foothold in Greece's Parliament earlier this summer, 50 of its members riding motorbikes and armed with heavy wooden poles roared through Nikaia, a gritty suburb west of [Athens], to telegraph their new power.

As townspeople watched, several of them said in interviews, the men careened around the main square, some brandishing shields emblazoned with swastikalike symbols, and delivered an ultimatum to immigrants whose businesses have catered to Nikaia's Greeks for nearly a decade.

"They said: 'You're the cause of Greece's problems. You have seven days to close or we'll burn your shop—and we'll burn you,'" said Mohammed Irfan, a legal Pakistani immigrant who owns a hair salon and two other stores. When he called the police for help, he said, the officer who answered said they did not have time to come to the aid of immigrants like him.

Golden Dawn denied any of its members were involved in the threats in Nikaia. Meanwhile, HRW reports that immigrants interviewed in Greece said they won't go out at night for fear of assault and attack by "often black-clad groups of Greeks intent on violence."

Austerity and a continuing economic depression has crippled Greece, and as the summer continues, so has the uptick in xenophobic violence and governmental discrimination—curious, as Golden Dawn is a favored party of "many police officers . . . and disaffected youth," according to the *Chicago Tribune*. There have also been reports of a "fascist element" in the Greek police and deep connections to Golden Dawn for years. An op-ed from [Arab news network] Al Jazeera also alleges Golden Dawn's police connection and describes their modus operandi.

"They terrorize immigrants, leftists, and journalists; they beat and maul teachers and students; they have infiltrated athletic clubs and have introduced hooliganism to the Greek landscape; and they have assumed the role of vigilantes," wrote Greek anthropologist Neni Panourgia in May. "Police brutality, hooliganism, and the deep-seated intimacy between fragments of the police force and Golden Dawn have made the organisation's temporary surge possible."

However, although reports of Golden Dawn members being complicit in street justice in Greece continue, there is no proof the party is actually behind the attacks, sanctioning them, or directing them, said HRW.

Anti-Semitism in Romania

The Anti-Defamation League [ADL] called on a Romanian lawmaker last week to apologize for what the ADL is calling "Holocaust denial."

Dan Sova, the newly appointed Minister for Parliamentary Relations, said "no Jew suffered on Romanian territory" during World War II, to the shock and dismay of many in the Jewish community in Romania and abroad. Sova was apparently sent on a field trip to the Holocaust museum, but has yet to publicly apologize for his remarks, according to Israeli news outlet Arutz Sheva.

Arutz Sheva also reported that Jewish parliamentarian Aurel Vainer called Sova "unsuitable for the job," and said she is "willing to wear a black band around my arm [in protest]."

Anti-Semitism is just one of Romania's problems as anti-Roma actions continue and the government turns a blind eye to the massive issues in the ghettos.

When the Roma go back to their countries of origin from places like France (see above), more problems arise: the ghettos in cities like Bucharest are even worse than the Western European camps, according to a recent op-ed by Valeriu Nicolae, founder of the Policy Centre for Roma and Minorities. The instances of HIV/AIDS is increasing, he said, as well as crime and illiteracy. There is little incentive for Roma to leave France [and] return to the East, where they are a despised ethnic minority and face terrible violence and discrimination, which has only increased in recent years.

But most of the serious anti-Roma action comes from Romania's neighbor to the West, Hungary.

Racism and Violence in Hungary

In July, a mob descended on the small village of Devecser (famous for the 2010 sludge flood) after a 2,000-person Jobbik rally took place in the square there. The predominately Roma-populated village was an obvious choice for a rally of nationalist white supremacists, and Amnesty International reports eyewitnesses said "some members of the crowd chanted anti-Roma slogans and threw pieces of concrete and other missiles at Roma houses. The police did not act to stop the violence and it is unclear whether any arrests were made."

Amnesty called on the Hungarian government to crack down on policing Jobbik and vigilantes aligned with the party, which rose to prominence in the past few years. But there has been little movement besides a softly-worded response from the Prime Minister's office, according to *Politics.hu*, an English-language news site.

"One activist told Amnesty International that she was in the courtyard of one Roma house when it was attacked," says Amnesty's report of the incident. "The crowd started chanting anti-Roma slogans and threw bottles, stones and pieces of concrete. She was hit in the arm and injured by a piece of concrete and has since filed a criminal complaint with the police."

Hungary is also still reeling from the whiplash-inducing 180-degree turn by Szegedi, who like any good politician, will now look into better understanding his Jewish roots. But don't get excited, he's not totally reformed from [being a] right-wing anti-Semite. According to the AP, Szegedi is quoted as saying he just defines himself as having "ancestry of Jewish origin—because I declare myself 100 percent Hungarian." Because you can't be both, apparently.

> *"Jews have much more to fear from the European left than they do from the European far right."*

The European Left Is More Dangerous to Jews than Is the European Right

Soeren Kern
Originally published by Gatestone Institute

Soeren Kern is senior fellow for transatlantic relations at the Strategic Studies Group, a think tank in Madrid, Spain. In the following viewpoint, he argues that it is the Left in Europe, not the Far Right, that is the real danger to Jews and Israel. He says that liberals demonize Israel and support the Palestinian cause against Jews and that the Left in Europe encourages and supports Muslim immigration, and he blames Muslim immigrants for most anti-Semitic violence in Europe. On the other hand, he argues that some far-right parties are strong supporters of Israel and strong opponents of Islam.

As you read, consider the following questions:

1. How does Kern say that modern anti-Semitism is generally disguised?

Soeren Kern, "European Left Is More Dangerous for Jews than the European Right," Gatestone Institute, June 17, 2009. www.gatestoneinstitute.org. Copyright © 2009 by Gatestone Institute. All rights reserved. Reproduced by permission.

2. Why were the findings of the EUMC report on anti-Semitic violence embarrassing to the Left, according to the author?

3. In which countries does Kern feel that far-right groups are animated by common sense?

Jewish groups in Europe and the United States have reacted with alarm to the gains made by far-right political parties in the recent elections for European Parliament. Right-wing and nationalist parties posted significant victories in Austria, Britain, Denmark, Hungary, Romania and the Netherlands in four days of voting that ended on June 7 [2009].

A Disturbing Trend

The Paris-based European Jewish Congress (EJC), an umbrella organization for Jewish communities in Europe, said: "As we assess the results of this week's elections, one disturbing trend has already crystallized; the gains made by extreme-right groups is a Europe-wide phenomenon. The success of the far-right and nationalistic parties that won seats in the elections on the basis of racist, anti-Semitic and xenophobic platforms points to a clear erosion of tolerance and a clarion call to European officials to immediately engage in intercultural dialogue. The success of such rabid groups as The Freedom Party in the Netherlands, the Freedom Party in Austria (FPO), the Danish People's Party, the British National Party, and Jobbik in Hungary, among others, will sadly only serve to embolden those who espouse the dangerous concepts of extreme nationalism, racism, anti-Semitism and xenophobia."

The New York–based Anti-Defamation League (ADL) said it was "deeply distressing that the blatantly anti-Semitic parties received so many votes," and called on European leaders to "ensure that anti-Semitism, racism and bigotry never again gain a foothold in Europe. . . . It is imperative that European

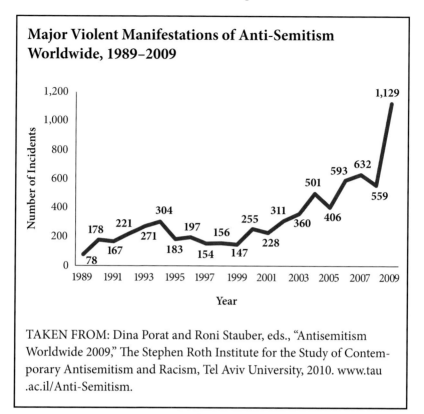

Major Violent Manifestations of Anti-Semitism Worldwide, 1989–2009

TAKEN FROM: Dina Porat and Roni Stauber, eds., "Antisemitism Worldwide 2009," The Stephen Roth Institute for the Study of Contemporary Antisemitism and Racism, Tel Aviv University, 2010. www.tau .ac.il/Anti-Semitism.

leaders do not remain silent, but speak out and reject the hateful and bigoted worldview of parties of the far-right and their supporters."

The Geneva-based World Jewish Congress (WJC) said: "Far-right parties and extremists have made gains across Europe amid protest votes and low turnout for the European Parliament (EP) elections. The elections were held in all 27 EU [European Union] member states from Thursday to Sunday last week [first week of June 2009]. Support for centre-Left parties and governments collapsed across the EU as fringe parties picked up protest votes."

Although these and other Jewish groups are not alone in their concerns about rising anti-Semitism in Europe, their fear of the far right often obscures the indisputable fact that some of the greatest threats to Jews (and Israel) in contemporary Europe stem from the left side of the political aisle. Indeed, it is no big secret that all across the European continent, left-wing intellectuals are playing a crucial role in making anti-Semitism seem respectable. Of course, they are (usually) careful to promote their hatred of Jews only indirectly. Instead, modern anti-Semitism is typically disguised as anti-Zionism and an obsession with Palestinian victimhood.

Judeophobia Is Supported by the Left

European Judeophobia often takes on new life forms such as anti-Semitic boycott campaigns and anti-Israel demonstrations, the growing intensity of which the European left not only overlooks or obscures but often actively supports. It is transmitted by Europe's left-leaning mass media, which not only believes that the systematic demonization of Israel promotes the postmodern and postnational ideological worldview of Europe's governing class, but also appeases the wrath of Europe's Muslim immigrants, lest they expose the myth of European socialist multicultural utopia.

As the European left intensifies its common cause with the Palestinian movement, Islam itself has emerged as a major threat to Jewish life in Europe. Although definitive statistics are scarce, most of the acts of violence against Jews and Jewish institutions in Europe in recent years seem to be perpetrated by Muslim extremists. Indeed, a 2003 report published by the European Monitoring Center on Racism and Xenophobia (EUMC) attributed the increase in anti-Semitic violence in Europe mainly to Muslims and pro-Palestinian groups. But those findings were so embarrassing that European left-wing elites quashed the report and commissioned another one. A subsequent EUMC report, which used a more politically correct research methodology, concluded that the "noticeable rise in reported anti-Semitic incidents" was the fault of "young, white Europeans incited by traditional right-wing extremist groups."

In any case, right-wing groups such as Geert Wilders's Party for Freedom in the Netherlands and the Danish People's Party, far from being the purveyors of "rabid" racism and anti-Semitism that the EJC claims, are some of the best allies that Jews (and Israel) will find in Europe today. In fact, the Danish People's Party is a strong supporter of Israel as well as the US-led War on Terrorism, of which Israel is a major beneficiary. It has called for stronger sanctions against totalitarian regimes and dictatorships, especially those in the Islamic world. It has also supported academic grants for specific research into terrorism and Islamism. For his part, Wilders calls himself a true friend of Israel. During a recent visit to Jerusalem, Wilders said: "We see Christians and Jews as part of one culture. When I'm here I'm with my people, my country, my values. I feel more at home here than in many other European countries. Israel's a democracy—it's everything we stand for."

Against Multicultural Dogma

Wilders and a growing number of other Europeans understand the threat that Islam poses to Europe and to the Western world. They are also taking a stand against a European left-wing political class that despises its Judeo-Christian heritage so much that it has become an undiscerning apologist for Islam. Unfortunately, the Islamization of Europe, which is being promoted by an intolerant left-wing multicultural dogma that gives immigrants more rights than natives, is one of the main factors contributing to the alarming rise of truly troublesome extremist groups like the Hungarian Jobbik party.

The European political right is far more nuanced and complex than catch-all labels such as "far right" or "extreme right" imply. Whereas right-wing groups in Denmark and Holland, animated by common sense, are pushing back against a European multicultural movement that has run amok and has pushed Western Civilization to the edge of the abyss, other groups like those in Austria, Hungary and Romania, animated by ignorance, are promoting hatred against any and all immigrants just for the sake of it. It is a world of difference.

The knee-jerk tendency to stereotype the European right-wing as anti-Semitic obscures the fact that, with few exceptions, the only genuine European supporters of Jews and Israel are on the political right-wing. Indeed, in the bigger scheme of things, Jews have much more to fear from the European left than they do from the European far right.

Periodical and Internet Sources Bibliography

The following articles have been selected to supplement the diverse views presented in this chapter.

Max Bohnel and Ingar Solty	"Right-Wing Populism and the Republican Party," Global Research, September 4, 2012. www.globalresearch.ca/right-wing-populism-and-the-republican-party/5303158.
Frida Ghitis	"Europe's Blind Spot on Anti-Semitism," CNN.com, March 23, 2012. www.cnn.com/2012/03/22/opinion/ghitis-toulouse-palestinian/index.html.
Daniel Greenfield	"The Democratic Party and Jewish Anti-Semitism," Accuracy in Media, April 5, 2012. www.aim.org/guest-column/the-democrat-party-and-jewish-anti-semitism.
Abe Greenwald	"Occupy Wall Street Has an Anti-Semitism Problem," *Commentary*, October 11, 2011.
Lord Sacks	"Europe's New Anti-Semitism," *Huffington Post*, July 11, 2012. www.huffingtonpost.com/chief-rabbi-lord-sacks/europe-new-anti-semitism_b_1663157.html.
Colin Shindler	"The European Left and Its Trouble with Jews," *New York Times*, October 27, 2012. www.nytimes.com/2012/10/28/opinion/sunday/europes-trouble-with-jews.html?pagewanted=all.
Keno Verseck	"Hungary's Far-Right Rhetoric Reaches New Dimension," *Spiegel Online*, November 28, 2012. www.spiegel.de/international/europe/far-right-rhetoric-in-hungary-reaches-new-dimension-a-869826.html

For Further Discussion

Chapter 1

1. Is anti-Semitism a constant, unchanging force, or does it alter depending on circumstances? Cite from the viewpoints in this chapter to support your answer.

Chapter 2

1. How is the tone of Pieter van der Horst's comments about Christian anti-Semitism different from the tone of Andrew Bostom's viewpoint about the anti-Semitism in Islam? Which viewpoint is more convincing in its argument that the religion in question (either Christianity or Islam) has a history of anti-Semitism? Why?

2. Phyllis Chesler says that opposition to Muslims is not Islamophobia because Muslims really do pose a danger to Europe. Would Sabine Schiffer and Constantin Wagner agree with the logic behind her statement? Why or why not?

Chapter 3

1. Which of the other authors in the chapter would David Solway consider to be anti-Semites? On what grounds? Cite evidence from the viewpoints.

2. Spencer Ackerman says that "Israel Firster" was a term first used by white supremacists. Does Philip Weiss address this charge? Do you think he would consider it sufficient reason to stop using the term? Why or why not?

Chapter 4

1. Richard Cohen suggests that people should be outraged by false charges of anti-Semitism. Do you agree with him? Why or why not?

2. On the basis of the viewpoints by Alex Pearlman and Soeren Kern, which seems more dangerous, the anti-Semitism of the European right or the anti-Semitism of the European left? Why?

Organizations to Contact

The editors have compiled the following list of organizations concerned with the issues debated in this book. The descriptions are derived from materials provided by the organizations. All have publications or information available for interested readers. The list was compiled on the date of publication of the present volume; the information here may change. Be aware that many organizations take several weeks or longer to respond to inquiries, so allow as much time as possible.

Aish International
1 Western Wall Plaza, PO Box 14149, Jerusalem 9114101
  Israel
+972 73 229-3400 • fax: +972 2 627-3172
e-mail: webmaster@aish.com
website: www.aish.com

Aish International is a conservative religious organization that operates learning centers in various locations throughout the world, including Jerusalem. Aish runs educational and religious programs aimed at fostering traditional Jewish values and beliefs. The organization maintains extensive online resources at its website, including articles such as "Combating Anti-Semitism" and "Denying Muslim Anti-Semitism."

American Israel Public Affairs Committee (AIPAC)
251 H Street NW, Washington, DC 20001
e-mail: information@aipac.org
website: www.aipac.org

The American Israel Public Affairs Committee is dedicated to strengthening the ties between the United States and Israel. It works to educate and lobby decision makers about pro-Israel policies. It publishes the biweekly *Near East Report*, the triannual *Israel Connection*, and the monthly one-page *Middle East Spotlight* e-bulletin. These publications and others are available through AIPAC's website.

American Jewish Committee (AJC)
PO Box 705, New York, NY   10150
(212) 751-4000 • fax: (212) 891-1450
e-mail: newyork@ajc.org
website: www.ajc.org

The American Jewish Committee is an international think tank and advocacy organization supporting Israel's efforts for peace and security, as well as strengthening American Jews' ties to Israel and combating bigotry and anti-Semitism. The organization runs public awareness and education campaigns and community events to bring about these goals. The AJC publishes *The American Jewish Year Book* annually, as well as articles on subjects such as Jewish life, the Holocaust, and Israel on its website.

Anti-Defamation League (ADL)
PO Box 96226, Washington, DC   20090
(202) 452-8310 • fax: (202) 296-2371
e-mail: washington-dc@adl.org
website: www.adl.org

The Anti-Defamation League is a nonprofit advocacy group that seeks to end discrimination against Jews—and all people—through the collection and dissemination of information about anti-Semitism, bigotry, and prejudice. The ADL publishes an annual report detailing its findings, the monthly newsletter *Connections*, the *International Report*, and the security report *On Guard*.

International Fellowship of Christians and Jews (IFCJ)
30 N. LaSalle Street, Suite 4300, Chicago, IL   60606
(800) 486-8844
e-mail: info@ifcj.org
website: www.ifcj.org

The fellowship works to promote greater understanding between Christians and Jews and to build support for Israel. The IFCJ publishes press releases and editorials on several topics, including the religious persecution of Jews and Christians. Many of these are available through the IFCJ website.

J Street

PO Box 66073, Washington, DC   20035
(202) 596-5207
e-mail: info@jstreet.org
website: http://jstreet.org

J Street is an advocacy group that works to promote American leadership in ending the Arab-Israeli conflict. J Street supports a two-state solution and a peaceful and diplomatic resolution to conflicts. The organization's website includes a blog, policy positions, press releases, and other articles and briefings focused on US-Israel policy.

Partners for Progressive Israel

114 W. 26th Street, Suite 1002, New York, NY   10001
(212) 242-4500 • fax: (212) 242-5718
e-mail: mail@meretzusa.org
website: http://partners4israel.org

Partners for Progressive Israel (formerly Meretz USA) is a liberal nonprofit organization that supports peace between Israel and its neighbors, including the Palestinians, and social justice for all of Israel's inhabitants. The organization seeks to draw awareness to the issue of conflict in the Middle East through rallies, public awareness campaigns, and lectures. Its website includes a blog, articles, and other resources.

Simon Wiesenthal Center

1399 S. Roxbury Drive, Los Angeles, CA   90035
(310) 553-9036; toll-free: (800) 900-9036 • fax: (310) 553-4521
e-mail: webmaster@wiesenthal.com
website: www.wiesenthal.com

The Wiesenthal Center works to fight anti-Semitism and bigotry around the world. It operates Museums of Tolerance in Los Angeles, Jerusalem, and New York, as well as a film division, Moriah Films, to educate audiences about the Jewish experience. It maintains a resource center of materials on the Holocaust, twentieth-century genocides, anti-Semitism, racism, and related issues, which it makes available to students. Its website includes news items, articles, and op-eds on topics such as anti-Semitism and Jewish policy.

Vidal Sassoon International Center for the Study of Antisemitism
Hebrew University of Jerusalem
Mount Scopus Campus, Jerusalem   91905
   Israel
+972 2 588-2494 • fax: +972 2 588-1002
e-mail: sicsa@mail.huji.ac.il
website: http://sicsa.huji.ac.il

The Sassoon center is an interdisciplinary research institution dedicated to understanding anti-Semitism. The center engages in research on anti-Semitism, focusing on relations between Jews and non-Jews in situations of tension and crisis. It publishes numerous papers, books, articles, and reports on anti-Semitism, many of which are available thorugh its website.

World Jewish Congress
501 Madison Ave., New York, NY   10022
(212) 755-5770
e-mail: info@worldjewishcongress.org
website: www.worldjewishcongress.org

The World Jewish Congress is an international nongovernmental organization that aims to promote the needs of Jews around the world. It has a diplomatic seat at the United Nations where it works to ensure that its goal of security and peace for Jewish communities is met. Its website includes issue papers, news, reports, and other resources.

Bibliography of Books

Stephen E. Atkins   *Encyclopedia of Right-Wing Extremism in Modern American History.* Santa Barbara, CA: ABC-CLIO, 2011.

Peter Beinart   *The Crisis of Zionism.* New York: Times Books, 2012.

Andrew G. Bostom   *The Legacy of Islamic Antisemitism: From Sacred Texts to Solemn History.* Amherst, NY: Prometheus Books, 2008.

Matti Bunzi   *Anti-Semitism and Islamophobia: Hatreds Old and New in Europe.* Cambridge, UK: Prickly Paradigm Press, 2007.

Avner Falk   *Anti-Semitism: A History and Psychoanalysis of Contemporary Hatred.* Westport, CT: Praeger, 2008

Tarek Fatah   *The Jew Is Not My Enemy: Unveiling the Myths That Fuel Muslim Anti-Semitism.* Toronto: McClelland & Stewart, 2011.

Norman G. Finkelstein   *Beyond Chutzpah: On the Misuse of Anti-Semitism and the Abuse of History.* Berkeley: University of California Press, 2005.

Robert O. Freedman, ed.   *Israel and the United States: Six Decades of US-Israeli Relations.* Boulder, CO: Westview, 2012.

Phyllis Goldstein	*A Convenient Hatred: The History of Antisemitism*. Brookline, MA: Facing History and Ourselves, 2012.
Bernard Harrison	*The Resurgence of Anti-Semitism: Jews, Israel, and Liberal Opinion*. Lanham, MD: Rowman and Littlefield, 2006.
David I. Kertzer	*The Popes Against the Jews: The Vatican's Role in the Rise of Anti-Semitism*. New York: Vintage Books, 2002.
Deepa Kumar	*Islamophobia and the Politics of Empire*. Chicago: Haymarket Books, 2012.
Walter Laqueur	*The Changing Face of Anti-Semitism: From Ancient Times to the Present Day*. New York: Oxford University Press, 2006.
Michael Lerner and Cornel West	*Jews and Blacks: A Dialogue on Race, Religion, and Culture in America*. New York: Plume, 1996.
Albert S. Lindemann	*Esau's Tears: Modern Anti-Semitism and the Rise of the Jews*. New York: Cambridge University Press, 1997.
Albert S. Lindemann and Richard S. Levy	*Antisemitism: A History*. New York: Oxford University Press, 2010.
John J. Mearsheimer and Stephen M. Walt	*The Israel Lobby and U.S. Foreign Policy*. New York: Farrar, Straus & Giroux, 2007.

Francis R. Nicosia *Zionism and Anti-Semitism in Nazi Germany.* New York: Cambridge University Press, 2008.

David Patterson *A Genealogy of Evil: Anti-Semitism from Nazism to Islamic Jihad.* New York: Cambridge University Press, 2010.

Dennis Prager and Joseph Telushkin *Why the Jews? The Reason for Antisemitism.* New York: Touchstone/Simon & Schuster, 2003.

Jack Ross *Rabbi Outcast: Elmer Berger and American Jewish Anti-Zionism.* Washington, DC: Potomac Books, 2011.

Robin Shepherd *A State Beyond the Pale: Europe's Problem with Israel.* London: Orion, 2009.

Colin Shindler *Israel and the European Left: Between Solidarity and Delegitimization.* New York: Continuum, 2012.

Joshua Trachtenberg *The Devil and the Jews: The Medieval Conception of the Jew and Its Relation to Modern Anti-Semitism.* 2nd ed. Philadelphia: Jewish Publication Society, 2002.

Robert S. Wistrich *From Ambivalence to Betrayal: The Left, the Jews, and Israel.* Lincoln: University of Nebraska Press, 2012.

Index

G

H